Shattered Hearts: A Personal Narrative

Shattered Hearts:
A Personal Narrative

By

Morgan Castle

Library and Archives Canada Cataloguing in Publication

Title: Shattered hearts : a personal narrative / Morgan Castle.

Names: Castle, Morgan, author.

Description: Translation of: Bienvenue en Afrique.

Identifiers: Canadiana (print) 20210233796
Canadiana (ebook) 20210235853

ISBN 9781771616003 (softcover) ISBN 9781771616010 (PDF)
ISBN 9781771616027 (EPUB) ISBN 9781771616034 (Kindle)

Subjects: LCSH: Castle, Morgan—Family. | LCSH: Adoptive parents—Canada— Biography. | LCSH: Adoption—Canada. | LCGFT: Autobiographies..

Classification: LCC HV874.82.C37 A3 2021
DDC 362.734092—dc23

Published by Mosaic Press, Oakville, Ontario, Canada, 2021.

MOSAIC PRESS, Publishers
www.Mosaic-Press.com

Printed and bound in Canada.

Cover Design by Rahim Piracha

Funded by the Government of Canada
Financé par le gouvernement du Canada

MOSAIC PRESS
1252 Speers Road, Units 1 & 2, Oakville, Ontario, L6L 5N9
(905) 825-2130 • info@mosaic-press.com • www.mosaic-press.com

Dedication

To Daniel, whom I will love forever.
Thank you for your never-ending support and love

Epigram

YOU WILL LOSE SOMEONE YOU can't live without, and your heart will be badly broken, and the bad news is that you never completely get over the loss of your beloved. But this is also the good news. They live forever in your broken heart that doesn't seal back up."

– Anne Lamott

Table of Contents

PROLOGUE

IT WAS JUST BARELY 10:00AM but it already seemed to be the longest day of our lives and. Every second seemed to drag on forever as we forced ourselves to go through our regular daily routine. Our appointment was for 4:00pm. We would have to leave work by 3:10pm to make sure we'd get there in time. The rest of our day was painstakingly slow, but somehow we managed to make it through without allowing our anxieties to get the best of us.

The drive was intense. Daniel's knuckles were as white as snow against the steering wheel. It was obvious he was as nervous as I was. No surprise really. Our entire future hung in the balance of this one meeting. We tried to make small chat—trying to ignore the excruciating tension as we drove in an otherwise awkward silence. Forty minutes after leaving work we finally pulled into the parking lot.

My heart pounded in my chest as we circled for a place to park. There were no available spaces in the primary lot. I wanted to throw up. It would only be a matter of minutes before our lives would change forever. That's a lot of pressure, even for two professionals who deal with multiple issues on a daily basis.

Don't hold your breath. Breathe. Concentrate on slowing down your heart rate. I was going to hyperventilate.

As we pulled into the nearest parking spot in the secondary parking lot we looked at each other. This was it. I was grinning—rather awkwardly—like someone who had returned from the dentist and was still frozen. Breathe.

Daniel turned the engine off. The keys rattled in his hands. He was as nervous as I was. I took hold of his hand. "Breathe?" I asked him. "Breathe," he responded, giving my hand a reassuring squeeze. Deep breaths.

We stepped out of our vehicle and walked toward the building. My body wanted to sprint. I wanted to get inside and hear the decision. I reached out and grabbed Daniel's hand again. Together we walked through the door and into the meeting. Neither of us was prepared for what would happen next.

CHAPTER 1

WAITING

HOW LONG HAD IT BEEN? Daniel checked his watch again. Another ten minutes had passed. We had not arrived early. We had arrived exactly on time. That had almost killed me. I am early by nature—but with heavy traffic and no immediate parking spaces, we had crossed the threshold at exactly 4:00PM.

Probably just as well. Early would be perceived as too eager—impatient even; and late would look unprofessional and irresponsible. Perhaps traffic and parking issues were divine intervention by some greater power. Let's hope so. Daniel and I were praying for as much divine intervention as we could get.

It had been a quick process to date—only three meetings. But arranging those meetings had taken a long time and organizing dates and times had proven no easy task. A process that had begun on December 10th was approaching its first crossroad in March. March 12th to be exact. That date will remain in my memory forever.

Anyone in the system would attest to this time frame as being record-breakingly fast. It probably was. But from our perspective—it was a long time to hold your breath. Another deep breath. Exhale. Just exhale.

I tried to calm my heart once again. It was raging inside my chest. With each passing moment it beat louder and louder, as if wanting to announce our presence. It wasn't as if we needed to be announced. The nonchalant receptionist had glanced up at us over the top of her outdated glasses. She gave us what I could only guess was a smile and looked back down at her work—or her fingernails—who knew?

As if reading my mind Daniel reached for my hand again. He had been doing that a lot lately. He was as invested in this as I was. That's an unnecessary understatement. We were equally invested in this. Both of us having prayed for this very moment for what seemed like an eternity. Actually this prayer was more like a revision of our original prayer.

Originally we had prayed to have our own biological child. We hadn't just prayed. We had seen every specialist we could, and had undergone multiple procedures, each in an attempt to create a little life. No such luck.

Invitro was out of the question. Not that we hadn't considered it—we had. But we had been told that such a process was against the catholic religion. That it was sinful to create life outside of the physical act of love, and that it was even more sinful if any fertilized eggs were discarded during the process. Another dead end.

We had discussed adoption many times. We had gone around and around the pros and cons. We had gone on websites, visited support groups, sought council from family, friends and clergy. Big decision. Big decision.

Am I babbling? I'm babbling. 4:20pm. Twenty minutes. That's late. Did I get the time wrong? No. Not possible. I'm anal to a fault. Besides, I would not mix up something this important. So. Twenty minutes late. What did that mean? Could be a good sign; then again, could be a bad sign.

Good things come to those who wait. Another deep breath. We waited. We exchanged glances. Daniel would squeeze my hand and I would glance up at him, then to the clock, then to the door, and back to the wall, or the floor, I wasn't sure where I was looking.

I really wasn't looking anywhere. I was reliving everything we had been through to date. The decision was difficult. We went around and around. Adopt. Wait. Leave it in God's hands. Round and around we went. And we didn't so much make the decision ourselves. Regardless of what happens next—I swear to you the decision was His.

I had been waiting for my class. I was standing outside the music room enjoying the sounds coming from inside. My class was not the best sounding class in the school, but they tried. I loved listening to them sing. Probably because I loved to sing myself.

The kindergarten children were lined up in the hallway having their bathroom break and getting drinks before heading back to class. Nothing out of the ordinary. This was the routine every second day. I smiled and made small talk with the children. I was familiar to them. I had taken them to our computer lab a few times so far this year. That's when it happened.

The door opened and jolted me from my memories. I almost jumped out of my skin. This was it. I squeezed Daniel's hand. To this day I do not know how I didn't break it. I stood up. Daniel pulled gently on my hand and I looked down at him. Breathe. He shook his head and guided me gently back to my seat. Not who we were waiting for. The receptionist glanced up at us again. This time she seemed to roll her eyes at us. I was probably overreacting. I was on edge.

Back to the music room. I love that memory. I had been talking to one of the Kindergarten teachers when he caught my eye. He had stepped up to the fountain and was taking a drink. I don't know why that caught my eye. That was par for the course. I turned my head to glance at him as I continued my conversation with the other teacher.

How adorable. His black hair was slicked back neat and tidy on his head. "Who's the little fella with the slicked back hair?" I had inquired. I was still smiling. Something about him made me smile.

Another squeeze of my hand. I looked at Daniel. He looked down at me and tried to smile. I love Daniel. He was as nervous as I was, but he was trying his best to be the strong one. He didn't need to. I was strong. I would handle whatever happened next. I just couldn't handle the waiting. That's where Daniel and I were different. He was better at the waiting. Another deep breath.

Back to the music room. I was still smiling. The Kindergarten teacher nodded in his direction without taking her eyes off me. "He's up for adoption," she replied matter- of-factly. That was the moment. Right there in that moment everything was clear. Adoption.

Daniel. I had to find Daniel. Before I could respond or gather my thoughts they were there. All twenty-something of them. Music had ended and it was time for our class. I walked them up to class. I don't remember doing it but I must have because the rest of the day passed quickly.

Daniel. I had to find Daniel. I almost tripped over myself getting to Daniel's class. Walk. No running in school. Although the day was over there were still a few students who had not left the building yet. Walk. Walk to Daniel's class.

My words were as fast as my heart. Daniel gripped my shoulders. Slow down. Of course he didn't understand the urgency. He didn't know what I knew. I asked him about the boy. Daniel worked with the Kindergarten class too. His class read with the Kindergarten children every now and then and Daniel prided himself on knowing each and every child in the class.

Daniel was amazing that way. He knew each and every student in the whole school. He loved kids. He always had. It was so clear now. Adoption.

I described the little boy to Daniel. He didn't know him. How could he not know him? Daniel knew every child in both Kindergarten classes. How could neither of us know him? It was nearly Christmas. It was odd that this child could have been in our school for that long and neither of us had seen him before.

The door opened again. This time it was her—our worker. I jumped to my feet. "We're not ready yet," she said. "He's not here." He would be our other worker. They always worked in pairs when assessing a couple for adoption. I sat back down. My nervousness was breaking Daniel's heart. Deep breath.

As miraculous as it was to have noticed him that day, that was not the biggest sign. The biggest sign came the next day. I was sure it had been a sign. I had prayed that night. It had been the first time in a long time. I had been sure that seeing the little boy had happened for a reason. But of course people can convince themselves of anything if they try hard enough.

We had almost given up on the idea of adoption. I couldn't remember the last time we had talked about it. Everything about that day had seemed like a sign. But, again, I didn't know if it was truly a sign, or if I just really, really wanted to believe it was a sign. So, I prayed.

I prayed for clarity. I prayed for forgiveness for not knowing if it was a sign. I also took the opportunity to remind Him that I was not a subtle person and so subtle signs would not work well with me. I prayed that if it had been a sign, could He please give me one more sign so I could be sure. Religious greed? That certainly wasn't my intention. I just needed to be sure.

Without hesitation my prayers were answered. This time the sign was not so subtle; not an off the cuff comment by a colleague. It had been parent teacher interviews. I was set up in the gym with the rest of the upper grade teachers. Daniel was in his classroom at the other end of the building, as were the rest of the lower grade teachers.

It had been a slow day. I was in the back corner of the gym and was pretty much secluded between parent visits. Daniel had popped down once or twice in the morning between his own visits. We were putting together plans and programs for the upcoming school months. We were both strong with time-management so we liked to make full use of our time.

Interviews were going well. Just two more before lunch break. I was debating between sneaking in a bathroom break or waiting until lunch. My bladder won and I closed over my books. I don't know what possessed me to take the long way to the staff bathrooms. It certainly wasn't my bladder. That was the beginning of what some would call a series of coincidences. You'll have to decide for yourself what you believe.

Coincident or not I passed the nearest stairway and headed down the hall. At the far end of the hall sat a young child. He was sitting on a chair outside the Kindergarten classroom. He was alone. His parent (or parents) must be inside in an interview. I thought little more of it. As I got closer to the middle stairway the child became more visible. This wasn't just any child. This was him. Of all the times to go to the washroom, of all the possible ways to get there, I had chosen this time and this route. Coincidence? Of all the children to be sitting outside of Kindergarten, of all the appointment times available, he was sitting there at exactly this time. Coincidence?

Maybe. Maybe all of it was coincidence. However I had asked for another sign less than 24 hours earlier. I find it hard to believe that that too would be coincidence. At some point this must go beyond coincidences. Besides that, what about the fact that the child had even been brought to interviews? That was not a common occurrence. Was that just another coincidence? And how exactly does one differentiate between coincidence and true signs?

Daniel. I had to get Daniel. He was probably in an interview. He had one scheduled for this time. If that was the case the boy would be gone before Daniel was free. I had to get Daniel.

"Hi," I said to the little boy as I walked swiftly past. I would have loved to stop and talk to him, as I would have with any of the other Kindergarten children had they been there. But I had to get Daniel.

Another door. I looked up. She was apologizing again for keeping us waiting. She had brought us each a small paper cup filled with luke warm water. She thought we might like a drink while we were waiting. Daniel was sure that was a good sign. I wasn't so sure. But, at this point my nervousness was getting the best of what was usually a strong gut instinct for situations like these.

Drink. It would be impolite not to. Don't want to be impolite with so much at stake. The water was warm.

It had that odd taste you get when you drink from a paper cup. It was hard to swallow. I finished the water and returned to my thoughts.

Daniel's door was open and he was not in an interview. I raced over to him and began dragging him into the hall as I hurriedly started explaining not only that the boy was right down the hall, but all the unexplained coincidences that had led me to see the boy in the first place. I was so excited I was spitting words like sign, faith, definite.

Daniel was calm. He wasn't always calm—at least not any more so than anyone else. But my excitement was probably enough for the both of us. Well, that and the fact that I was talking so fast and breathing so hard he probably had no idea what I was saying.

Daniel stood up. I looked up. He extended his hand for my cup. His hand was a little shaky. He was still as nervous as I was. Of course he was. Why wouldn't he be? People can only wait for so long before the waiting gets the best of them. He put the cups in the garbage can beside the reception's window. She didn't even glance up this time. He smiled at me as he returned to his seat and sat back down. I wound my arm around his and returned to my memories.

We weren't two steps out of Daniel's classroom before he noticed the little boy sitting quietly on the chair at the end of the hallway. It took no time for Daniel to put two and two together. When we got to the end of the hallway I hesitated. I had to get back to the gym for my next interview. I still hadn't used the bathroom. I decided I could hold off on the bathroom until lunch. I used my last two minutes to stay with Daniel and the little boy.

Daniel spoke to the little boy as he looked at the decorations on the tree beside the Kindergarten class. Daniel was by no means soft-spoken. His voice was as loud and energetic as he was. As he talked, the little boy peered at him from the corner of his eyes without lifting or turning his head. Daniel commented on how beautiful the decorations were and he proceeded to guess which one the little boy might have made. Although the children's names were visible on the back of each decoration, Daniel continued chatting as he looked them all over. The little boy didn't respond until Daniel reached his ornament. In an almost inaudible whisper the little boy said "that one's mine."

I smiled as I walked down the hallway toward the gym and back to my parent teacher interviews. Daniel had commended the little boy on such a beautiful ornament and asked if the ornament was made of felt in the boy's favorite colour. The boy whispered, again barely audible, a very soft-spoken "no." Daniel inquired as to the boy's favorite colour. The boy turned his head slightly to look up at Daniel and whispered "red." Daniel and the boy exchanged boyhood info such as favorite cartoon characters, favorite super heroes, and other such things.

After I finished my last parent teacher interview before lunch I went back to Daniel's room. I was dying to know what he thought. Did he think it had been a sign that the boy was there? Daniel was coming out of his room as I got to the door. We went upstairs to my room and spent the whole lunch hour talking about the boy and the possibilities. I still hadn't used the bathroom but somewhere along the way I had forgotten I needed to. I asked Daniel about his time with the little boy. I listened eagerly and hung on to every word he said. The most amazing part of Daniel's story actually took place after the little boy had left.

Daniel had returned to his own classroom for a parent teacher interview and then had been heading to the gym to see if I had finished my pre-lunch interview. On his way to the gym he met the Kindergarten teachers leaving their classroom. They were finished for the day and were heading home. It was great that Daniel had run into them. Daniel commented on meeting the little boy. The Kindergarten teachers inquired about Daniel's interactions with the boy and were shocked to discover the boy had actually spoken to Daniel. The little boy, for all intents and purposes, was believed to be selectively mute. To me this was yet another reaffirmation that things were happening for a reason.

On December 10th Daniel and I filled in an application to adopt the little boy. We had an appointment with the infertility doctor on that day. No new news. We were still labeled as unexplained infertility. There were no new procedures. We could retry some of the ones we'd already gone through, or re-consider invetro. That was about it.

It seemed like the perfect time. We were both ready and there was nothing happening biologically speaking. Besides that, we had both met the little boy and he had given us a whole new perspective on adoption.

We phoned the head office. We spoke to the head lady. We expressed our interest in adopting the little boy and inquired about the process. She explained that adopting this child would be considered a child-specific adoption. We would need to fill in an application. There was not much else that could be discussed until we filed the application.

We arrived at the office the next day. I had told the head lady when I had spoken to her on the phone, that we would be in sometime that week. She was unavailable to meet with us but had made sure to leave an application package with her receptionist. We were excited and nervous all at the same time. We couldn't wait to begin the process. I had taken the package from the receptionist. The envelope had our names printed neatly across the front.

Daniel and I took the application package to the lower level of the professional complex. There was a small cafeteria there. We sat at a table for two. It was in the far corner of the cafeteria. We read the adoption information booklet from cover to cover and then opened the application form. We spent over an hour going over the form and filling in the applicable information. There were many pages dedicated to researching what type of child the potential parents were interested in. Age. Sex. A huge section encompassing a check list depicting disabilities and disorders potential parents were willing to accept.

None of that was applicable to Daniel or me. We were not interested in creating a profile for some imaginary perfect child. We wanted to adopt the little boy. As big a decision as that was for us, it proved to be one of the easier aspects of the process. We could never have fathomed the things we would learn about the little boy, and how cruel people could be.

CHAPTER 2

THE VERDICT

"IT'S TIME," DANIEL SAID, STANDING up. I looked up. The man had arrived and was standing in the doorway waiting for us. We walked past the receptionist and into a maze of hallways and small, closet-sized rooms. We turned left and were steered into the first room on the right. It was a tiny room. Despite the yellow paint, the room had more of a clinical feel to it. There was a small couch on one side of the room no bigger than a love seat—Daniel and I sat there. There were two other chairs in the room. The man sat on the chair closest to the couch and the woman sat on the chair directly across from us. There was a coffee table in front of us and a small table with a lamp beside the chair the man was sitting on.

The tension was obvious. There was a box of tissue on the coffee table in front of us. Within arm's reach. I was hoping that was routine and not just placed in here for us. That would not be a good sign.

Things had been tense the first time we had met them. There was so much riding on that meeting. We had rushed down after work one afternoon and had squeezed into an office on the opposite side of the maze. They explained the process: the first meeting is to explain the process and allow us to ask questions, the second meeting is to find out about us, the third meeting is a home visit, and then a decision about continuing on to further steps.

It's almost impossible to act normal and give a true depiction of yourself under those circumstances. It's like trying to maintain a genuine smile when posing for a photograph.

When we left the first meeting we drove home in silence. The process itself was pretty straight forward, however in order to determine our commitment to this particular little boy, they wanted to ensure that we were aware of all the issues and challenges this little boy would present. Half way home I needed Daniel to pull over. I scrambled out of the vehicle and vomited onto the shoulder of the road.

I cannot begin to describe the horror that had been the little boy's life. Dear God. His challenges and issues paled in comparison to the things he had experienced in his short years on this Earth. I had been molested as a child. That was a trip to Disney compared to what the little boy had survived. My stomach churned, my throat burned, and my heart ached. My mind reeled. Only a monster could do such things to a child! Only a monster could allow such things to happen to their child!

There was not a doubt in my mind that Daniel and I together could provide the little boy with a stable and loving home. Provide him with a safe and loving environment in which he would learn to trust and to love. I also knew that would be no easy task. It would take a long, long time. Daniel and I would need a lot of support to ensure we offered this boy everything he would need from a forever home.

I scrambled back into the vehicle and put my seatbelt back on. Daniel reached over and squeezed my hand. I looked at him with tears streaking down my cheeks. "Me too," he said before I could say anything. "And, yes." Daniel knew me inside-out, as I did him. And, yes. Despite the challenges, yes.

They looked at us. The man was smiling as the woman began talking. She was holding the report they had generated from the information they had gathered during our sessions together. We had three—no more than four—sessions in total, although each session had well exceeded the scheduled hour.

I don't think I had endeared them to me in the first meeting. Daniel had definitely won them over, but I had not made the best of impressions. My analytical nature caused them some distress. At various times in the meeting they would exchange glances, or frown slightly, things of that nature. Not wanting any misconceptions, I inquired about their shared glances. Not my best move. Although, I do not see anything wrong with being upfront—especially when the rest of one's life is hanging in the balance.

I didn't realize I had come off so poorly until the second visit. The second visit would see them finish researching Daniel—asking questions about upbringing, siblings, family relationships, personal characteristics and qualities, etc.; and would continue with similar research about me.

The woman began with a recap of my analytical personality. That was when I figured out I had not been fondly received, to say the least. She inquired as to how I thought a young boy with special challenges would react to being analyzed all the time. I was caught off guard. I wanted to cry. I don't analyze children. Daniel jumped immediately to my defense. He had noticed their interactions during the last meeting and would have inquired about them as well, had I not done so first.

I don't think they bought it. They assumed they had Daniel pegged. Easy-going, athletic, a Leave It To Beaver dad. Not exactly. Daniel would certainly be a super father. But I think their perception was a bit too lofty. Daniel was a very intelligent and astute man. He was not always easy-going. He was passionate about his beliefs and did not sit back and let people walk over him. So, easy-going—not always. But in my mind that was not a downfall, it was just one of many of his strengths. Daniel was as passionate about family, traditions, and relationships as he was about soccer and baseball. Daniel would make a wonderful parent.

Then there was me. I am also a very passionate person. I am strong minded and strong willed. I am committed, devoted, and dedicated, and will go to great lengths to advocate for fairness and justice. Despite this description, I am not a loud-mouth blow bag. I am diplomatic in my interactions with people and am able to remain calm and level-headed when dealing with stressful situations and confrontations. I do, however, communicate openly which is not always a welcome strength. Especially not with her.

We butted heads. The more I tried not to butt heads, the more we butted heads. She was also a very strong willed, strong minded woman. I don't have any problem with that. I respect people who speak their mind. What I don't respect is people who make up their minds before considering all the facts.

She was not only assigned to our case, she was also the worker for the little boy's mother and siblings. She stated (on many occasions) her compassion and sympathies for the biological mother. I had never met the biological mother—obviously—but I really wasn't interested in hearing about compassion for a woman who had allowed what she had allowed. The woman did not like my frame of mind regarding the mother. Despite where my lack of open mindedness for his mother had gotten me, I still have not changed my mind on that.

The adoption of this little boy was to be "closed with openness". What this meant was that the little boy would remain in contact with his siblings, and, indirectly his mother. We did not have a problem with maintaining a relationship with his siblings. We wondered what this would look like. We asked about the details of such a relationship—how often, where, what was the attitude of the siblings toward the adoption of their brother, etc.

We were told that those questions were not our business. We were interested in adopting the little boy. His family was not our business. Interesting. So "closed with openness" must be a one way street. And how exactly can we agree to facilitate a relationship when we don't know what that would entail?

No. The answer was no. She said she wanted to do us the favor of getting to the bottom line and sparing us the pain of waiting for an answer. So, no. We were not successful candidates to be the little boy's family.

Daniel was shocked. I sat very quiet, listening. I wanted all the facts before launching into what would either be a defense or an attack. I was analyzing. I was analyzing all the facts to justify a response. Daniel was still in shock.

She continued. Our concern over the biological family made them uncomfortable. And because she was tied to the family she felt fully justified in concluding that our questions depicted reservations about the boy's family. Don't explode. Just listen—carefully. Take it all in. Remember it.

The successful parents will need to accept him and his family situation. I wanted to swear at her. I wanted to explode all over her about the difference between reservation and seeking clarity and understanding. I wanted to scream that Daniel and I could not possibly have agreed or disagreed with things as they had been mapped out.

Hostile. That was the word they had used. The siblings were not at all accepting of their brother being adopted. They would undermine the process and could potentially be hostile. Hostile as in phoning at all hours of the night, or hostile as in showing up on the doorstep drunk with a gun? To Daniel and I there was a huge distinction that needed to be made between which hostile we were referring to. And that did not suggest that we would not be able to handle either version of hostile, but we sure as hell wanted to be prepared for the right one. It'd be pretty hard to hang up on a gun in your face. See the dilemma?

Stay calm. "What about you Morgan? You seem really quiet Morgan. How are you feeling Morgan?" Okay—first, repeating my name in each short little sentence came across as patronizing. Second, are you kidding me? How am I feeling? Sarcasm. It was the nicest response I could muster. "Good to know," I said, trying to mimic Angelina Jolie in *Girl Interrupted.* Okay not the best role model in this situation, but please tell me you see why I'd go that route.

Daniel jumped in. I love Daniel. I smiled at his chivalry. He expressed a heartfelt sincerity that so long as the little boy had a good home, we would be happy for him. I admired Daniel. He was right. We would never begrudge the little boy his forever home. Yes it was disappointing that his forever home would not be with us, but the bottom line was that we wanted nothing more than for his happiness.

"Oh, we don't have anyone for him," she continued. "But I am 100% confident in my decision that it's not you." She looked from Daniel to me. I wanted to leap across the table. Don't leap across the table. That would not help.

I remained quiet and poised. Daniel was not so content now. "So you'd rather see him bounce from foster home to foster home until he's 18 than to have a life with us?"

"Yes," she replied again. She continued on about placements having broken down in the past and how detrimental that is to everyone involved. I imagine it would be. What I couldn't imagine was that a life with us would break down. Yes it would be challenging—for all of us, but it wouldn't break down. Daniel and I are both teachers. We deal with severe issues all the time. We work with families and counselors and outside agencies on a regular basis to improve the quality of life for our students and their families. I am the head of our special education department. I deal with special needs on a daily basis. I support students with special needs for a living.

CHAPTER 3

THE JUSTIFICATIONS

THE REST OF THEIR JUSTIFICATIONS were frustrating.

We were a young couple with no parenting experience. First of all we are not young. I am 35 and Daniel is 30. That is not young to be starting a family. Yes we had only been married for over two years, but we had been best friends and co-workers for years prior to that. Second, I don't see why being young—as they were suggesting—would be a downfall. Our age would be an asset. This little boy would have life-long needs. Our age would allow us to support him well into his adult-hood. How is this a bad thing?

We had no children and also no parenting experience. There are a ton of people with parenting experience who would have never experienced a child with similar needs to this little boy. They wanted to replicate his biological family and we could not offer him siblings, which, ironically, he had just mentioned wanting the day before last. Liar. In all our visits the only thing that had come up was the knowledge that the little boy wanted a mommy and a daddy. Suddenly he wants siblings and, coincidentally, we don't have any to offer him. I was having trouble buying the validity of this reasoning.

We had stress free lives and wouldn't be able to handle the stress that comes with being parents. Well that makes sense. We only teach large numbers of children for 6 hours each day—totally stress free. Definitely. Liar. Stress free? What part of our meetings had they not been listening to?

> *I had felt so badly for Daniel. His family was very private. He was brought up to keep issues in-house. This portion of the process had nearly killed him. He had to share very private and personal issues that concerned his family. Medical issues, issues dealing with terminal illness, financial issues with family members, alcohol issues and abuse in his extended family. I knew him so well. He felt as though he was betraying his family by airing their dirty laundry.*
>
> *My family history wasn't much brighter. Every family has skeletons in their closets somewhere along the way. My family was fortunate enough to have avoided issues of terminal illness, at least to date, but otherwise we were running par with Daniel's family. I also had a sibling struggling with mental and emotional issues.*

And somehow after all this the consensus that Daniel and I lead stress-free lives was determined and then used against us. The process was flawed. She did not want the boy with us. She was not thinking about the boy. She was thinking about the siblings and the biological mother.

"You do not have an extensive knowledge of his Native culture," she continued. I honestly think I hated her. Not because the answer was no. I could have handled that answer had it been decided in the best interest of the boy. But not in this case. In this case, something else was fueling her decision. I hated her.

"Native?" we had asked. We thought they had the wrong child. The little boy was not native. Was he? Not that it really mattered either way. We had grown to think of him as our potential child at that point. We didn't look at him in terms of cultures or differences. To us he was just a little boy who needed a stable and loving home. He was a little boy who we wanted to share our stable and loving home with.

"Yes. Native," they had replied. I think it was the man who had answered us that time. He was shocked that we hadn't realized it. Daniel and I are neither blind nor ignorant, but we hadn't realized that the boy was Native.

The boy's culture did not weigh into our decision at all. He was still the little boy to us. We would love him and raise him regardless of culture.

We openly and immediately made our intentions known to do our best to ensure he grew up aware of his culture. We were not overly knowledgeable in that area, but were more than willing to learn. We both had minimal experiences with the Native culture. I had taught in an Alternate school with a high population of students with Native heritage. We had studied it in our classes and incorporated many traditions into our school.

Daniel had gone to school with Native children.

"We would like the little boy to have a Native family, or a family more aware of the Native culture and customs." Her again. The man jumped in now. He wanted to let us know that they thought we were wonderful people who would make amazing parents. Amazing parents to any child except him. Except him. I hated her.

There was something mentioned about Daniel and I having lives that were too predictable. Lives that would not easily adapt to the unpredictably of a child. Some justification about our "nice, little trailer," being neat and tidy and something else about "everything in its place."

Daniel and I live in a mini-home. It's relatively new, less than three years old. The word "trailer" annoyed me. Something patronizing in her voice. I hated her. As for everything in its place, there are not too many other places when you live in a home that's as small and compact as a mini-home. So, yes. Neat and tidy. No shit. We knew they were coming. We wanted our home to be presentable.

"I'll vacuum," Daniel had said. He was wonderful that way. He usually reverted to vacuuming when I was in cleaning mode. We had taken the morning off work for the meeting. The woman was allergic to cats. We had 5 cats and a mini-schnauzer. We would have to put the cats in the bedroom and close the door. The dog could stay out with us. He was the world's cutest dog and was blessed with equally as cute a personality. We didn't want to lock him in a bedroom. Besides, he'd probably win them over.

Daniel and I had cleaned the house from top to bottom. I had wiped down all the hard surfaces and Daniel had even vacuumed all the furniture. Should be okay for her. We didn't want her to take an allergic reaction and need to cut the visit short.

I was pacing. The weather wasn't the best. It was snowing and there was a lot of slush on the roads. They were late. I had to be back to work for 12:00. It was my duty day. I had only booked off the morning. I'd have to answer their questions as succinctly as I could. I wouldn't have any extra time.

They finally arrived. They were nearly ½ hour late. The meeting would have to be cut short.

I would have to leave by 11:45am. They came in. Everything was clean, neat, and tidy. Everything was in its place.

Had I known then what I knew now I'd go back in time and leave a pile of dirty dishes in the sink. I'd scatter some clutter around and welcome them to a less than tidy home. Sometimes the best of intentions turn around and bite you square in the behind.

Then there was the fact that they felt Daniel and I had expectations that the little boy might not be able to live up to. Don't ask me what those expectations were as Daniel and I were not really sure what to expect. We knew that the road ahead would be bumpy, but our end goal was to grow into a happy and loving family. Is that too much to expect?

She had been all about analogies. Everything she discussed or explained was related back to an analogy. She discussed his life and his relationship with his siblings as pieces of yarn going this way and that. She emphasized how each added string would cause more and more tangles.

She had referred to him as being weighted down by a backpack jammed full of issues. She was hard to converse with. They had asked about our vision for a happy family. What had we dreamed of? What had we hoped for?

Daniel and I both responded identically the same. We hoped for a happy family. We did not have any expectations on particulars.

"What about secondary education?" they had asked. "Whatever he wants," we responded. "If he wants to be a doctor, we'll support him. If he wants to take a trade, we'll support him." We were completely open to whatever he would want.

It had been a trick question. They were not sure he would be capable of secondary education. That would have been fine with us too, that just wasn't what they had asked. Nice. How many strikes had this been for us? They asked us what we thought an evening would look like. We responded with things like, watching tv together, playing outside, learning various sports, jumping on the trampoline. We were met with adversity. "What if he doesn't want to do that?" We'd suggest something else. "What if he doesn't want to do that?" We suggest something else. This continued for a long time. For intelligent people Daniel and I weren't learning quickly. There was no right answer. This was another trick question.

So our expectations may be more than he was capable of. He would disappoint us. Our disappointment in him could crush him. This could all end in a breakdown. I felt like I was in an episode of *The Twilight Zone*. Were these people for real? Maybe this was a dream. I often dream about things I am fretting about.

I looked over at Daniel. He took my hand. This was not a dream.

These people were professionals, or so their training would suggest. Were they hoping we expected little to nothing from him? Every child has the right to be successful. Every child has the right to have someone believe in them. They were misunderstanding everything. We would support the little boy in whichever direction life took him—not pressure him with unrealistic expectations.

At this point there was nothing to say. I would listen now. I no longer needed to remind myself to be calm. It was obvious that their reasons were neither valid nor justified. Switch gears. Full steam ahead.

"Morgan," again the patronizing tone, "do you have anything to say?" This time I responded. "Who do we contact to appeal the decision?" The question was laced with ice. It wasn't anger. It was pure will and determination. A mistake had been made. Daniel and I would ensure it was rectified. Time to call in reinforcements.

CHAPTER 4

REINFORCEMENTS

"WHAT WOULD YOU APPEAL?" THIS time it was the man asking. "Your reasons for your decision," again ice cold. I was infuriated. I was done with these two people, but I was definitely not done moving forward. "Like what?" He tried to sound interested and upbeat. Maybe he was interested in discussing things and re-considering. I couldn't afford to trust him now. That ship had sailed.

"Like our lack of parenting experience," I suggested. I shared my viewpoint on that and suggested that all of their reasons could be considered from two, very opposite, viewpoints. "That doesn't matter," her again. I hated her. "I am 100% confident in my decision." I'd heard that already. Absolutely no willingness for discussion on her part. I hated her. "Would you like me to read you the whole report?" she snipped, as if attempting to justify her confidence in our apparently obvious lack of potential parenting skills. "No," I replied. I stretched out the word and left it hanging in the air etched in ice. Don't be snippy with me. In hindsight, perhaps "yes" would have been a better answer. It would have given Daniel and I more ammo with which to fight the decision. No point looking back.

Daniel could sense my increasing agitation with her. He stood. We were ready to go. I stood and began to follow him out of the room. The man thanked us for coming in. The lady said something, I don't know what. I had tuned her out. Not just her voice. Her. I was done with her. They smiled and offered us nice words of departure. I turned my back on them. "See ya," I tossed over my shoulder as I followed Daniel out of the closet-like room. That would be the last time we would see them.

We went out to supper. We had it already planned. Either a celebratory meal or a sympathy meal. Either way we knew we would not feel like cooking. I excused myself. I went to the ladies room. I sobbed. Only briefly. There wouldn't be a lot of time for tears. Daniel and I had work to do. "I love you," I whispered before leaving the stall. It was directed at the little boy.

Daniel knew instantly that I had been crying. He felt left out. I hadn't meant to leave him out. I just didn't want us to dwell on the negatives. I needed us to be ready to move forward. I knew if I broke down in front of him it would cripple us both and we couldn't afford the down time. As we picked at our meal we began to brain storm.

We compiled a list of people who knew us well. People who could attest to our true nature—despite what the man and woman had supposedly discovered. The adoption process was confidential. We could not share any information pertaining to the little boy. We wouldn't need to. We were not looking for people to attest to anything about the little boy. The people who knew us knew we could handle anything—and that included any and all issues that life with the little boy would present.

We would need to enlist the support of family, friends, and colleagues. These were the people who knew us best and knew our capabilities. They would be able to offer a perspective that was so obviously lacking from that of the man and woman.

Our parents. Yes biased—obviously. But they would have the most in-depth and intimate knowledge of us. My Aunt. She had worked for the system in the past and she knew and loved both Daniel and me. We each had an older sister. We relied on them as they knew us well and were both realistic. I had other siblings but they were consumed in personal issues of their own at the time. A friend who knew Daniel and I as individuals and as a couple. One colleague. That would be tough. We did not want to mix our personal and professional lives, but we knew we needed an unbiased perspective. It would be harder for someone to deny the words of someone who was not related to us.

We discussed several colleagues. Two were away. One was planning for a large celebration and we didn't want to rain on that parade. We picked the perfect colleague. She was kind and compassionate. She knew us both professionally. She knew our skills and abilities. She had seen us interact with children. She knew our strengths and our weaknesses. Her perspective would be most welcomed. And then, of course, ourselves. We too would submit a letter to the head lady. We would present our analysis of our abilities and our rationale for disputing the reasons the man and woman had denied our application.

Denied our application. That still stung. But more than stung—it burned. It burned deep inside. We knew it was wrong. We knew the wrong decision had been made. The burn was our fire. Our drive. We would not let this go. We would fight for the little boy. We would fight to give him the forever home he had been waiting for.

Daniel's parents were nervous. They didn't want to mess things up for us. Things were already messed up. Things couldn't get worse. Anything they had to say could only make things better. They needed to gather their thoughts. They had prayed for us many times. Never in their wildest dreams did they imagine they could do more than that.

Daniel's parents wrote the following:

To whom it may concern,

Our son Daniel will be married three years this summer. We were thrilled to learn that he and Morgan had applied to adopt a child. Daniel and Morgan are wonderful people who give so much of themselves to others in need and it would be wonderful to see them with a family of their own.

Our son has not always been the strong and confident person he is today. He had many struggles as a young child. He had difficulty with his speech and this seemed to have an affect on his self-esteem and his self confidence. When he entered the school system he grew to second guess himself and to falter under pressure. He was withdrawn in class and his speech was often referred to by his teachers when reporting his abilities.

As parents we were heart broken for our child and tried everything in our power to develop and maintain a sense of pride and confidence in this little child who we knew so well and loved so much. It was difficult to watch Daniel struggle with himself and not be able to do anything to fix it. We enrolled Daniel in Speech Therapy and encouraged a safe environment for him at home where he could be himself without worrying about making a mistake; saying something wrong; or getting caught up on his words. Despite the friends he had and the fun-loving nature he experienced at home, Daniel continued to be discouraged at school.

It was not until high school that Daniel began to realize who he was as a person and to develop as sense of pride and self-worth. Overnight Daniel blossomed into a confident and determined person who knew his own mind and was able to stand up for his self and the things he believed in. We were very proud of Daniel when he graduated top of his class and enrolled in University.

Daniel's choice to become a teacher made us proud. Daniel wanted to become a teacher to offer the support and encouragement to students that he felt he had missed out on in his early years. Daniel knew from his own experiences that he had a lot to offer, especially in terms of patience and understanding.

Daniel met Morgan through teaching and there have never been two other people more suited for one another. Both Daniel and Morgan are strong and positive individuals who encourage and inspire the people they come in contact with. They involve themselves in extracurricular activities to assist and support the students in their care. Running after school support groups, coaching various school sports, as well as facilitating school events and school development initiatives to enhance the lives of their students are all in a days work for our son and his wife.

A day rarely passes when we are in the community, whether it be getting groceries or paying bills, that we are not commended on the wonderful work and effort of Daniel and Morgan. They are well known and respected in the community for both their hard work and their dedication to the children.

Daniel and Morgan have equally as much time and effort for our family. They are a constant support for us, as well as for other family members. They are the first to offer support and the last to leave in times of need. Our family has experienced many ups and downs, and despite the challenges, Daniel and Morgan always remain upbeat and positive in the face of adversity.

It is without a shadow of a doubt that Daniel and Morgan would make wonderful parents. They possess, as individuals and as a couple, an extraordinary capacity to love and support the people closest to them. Any child, regardless of demographics or disposition, would be blessed to be a part of Daniel and Morgan's life.

Please contact us for any further information. We are not only confident, but assured in their potential as future parents.

Their words were beyond flattering. We were honored to have people think so highly of us. And to think they were nervous. Such compassionate words could never mess things up. We were forever indebted to the people who wrote letters on our behalf.

My parents were as discouraged and angered for Daniel and I as his parents had been. Our parents were wonderful people. They loved us and wanted the best for us. They were the type of people we aspired to be like, given the opportunity.

My parents wrote the following:

To Whom It May Concern,

The recent application by Daniel and Morgan has been rejected on what we believe to be groundless reasoning. It was determined that they are a young couple; yet, many people at slightly less than half their age begin their own families. Unfortunately today there are also many single teenage mothers who have children that they can neither support nor raise. These new mom's have no parenting or life skills, yet the child is not removed from their environment. There appears to be different rules for different people.

Secondly, it was also stated that they had "no parenting experience"! This is a bias remark when one considers the fact that both of these individuals are elementary teachers who have approximately 60 young children in their care seven hours per day and five days per week. We have witnessed how these young children willingly go to each of these teachers with not only their problems but their experiences as well.

We have seen their eyes light up when Daniel and Morgan enter a room. Morgan teaches and deals with children who have special needs which is an achievement in itself. Daniel and Morgan have met with families to counter these disabilities and to resolve problems for the betterment of the child. We have also met parents socially who simply could not stop praising Morgan and Daniel for their work with their children.

It was also noted that Morgan and Daniel live "stress free and predictable lives with high expectations"! Let me be the first to tell you that their lives are not "stress free" as we know these people better than anyone in your department! To provide further detail of these personal situations would violate the provisions of the privacy laws. I will state however, that no one would ever know when they are dealing with a stressful situation as it is not visible in their actions, mannerisms, or tone. There is absolutely nothing wrong to live a predictable life with high expectations! This not only gives one something to work and strive toward but it helps the person to rise above the norm. Attempting to better ones self is not a detrimental quality.

The aspect of "not having children of their own" appears to be a self defeating remark when one considers the fact that they have applied to adopt a child! A child would not have any better home to live in than with Daniel and Morgan. We know ten of their nieces and nephews not only love to visit them but want sleep overs and longer visit times. No matter where Daniel and Morgan are, these children will call out their names and run to them! We have never seen a child shy away from them!

Let it be known that Morgan is an extremely compassionate person who will not only help children but will and did assist adults. She has helped in areas where others would not. A few years ago her grandmother had suffered from a stroke. Morgan bathed her, cleaned her dentures, managed her medications, and constructed a series of words to practice helping in her speech recovery! Because of this help, it permitted us to take her out of a manor so that she could spend her last Christmas with her family.

Morgan taught in an "Alternate School" where she arranged and organized a trip to the far North for the students. This task was certainly above and beyond any work requirement. This opportunity provided a hands on experience for these children to see how others lived in the North. This endeavour did not end here as it also provided a means for the children of the North to visit and experience a more southern location. The second trip became a reality because of

Morgan's work as she arranged accommodations and planned several outings for these folks.

In conclusion we believe that a terrible injustice has happened here; not only to Morgan and Daniel, but to a child who may not be fortunate enough to receive a second chance.

I love my parents. The obvious fight in the letter was my dad. We were very similar in that way. We do not tolerate injustices very well. The many details and memories were my mom. Her compassionate nature would retain many of those amazing moments.

Both Daniel's sister and my sister were more than willing to write letters on our behalf. Neither needed any information from us. They knew almost instantly the things they wanted to say. Their letters were both completed within hours of our request.

My older sister wrote the following:

To whom it may concern,

This letter is an attestation to the character and qualities that Morgan and Daniel possess and how these qualities would support them in their role as parents. I am Morgan's older sister and have known her for her entire life. I am also a mother of three incredible little people and I know that parenthood is challenging and sometimes stressful, but is, without a doubt, the most wonderful experience life has to offer.

I truly believe that Morgan and Daniel would make incredible parents.

Individually they are each well-rounded people with an excellent balance of intelligence, logic, compassion, and love. One of Morgan's biggest assets is commitment. Once committed to something, she will give everything she has to see it through. She will use all resources and knowledge, but most importantly, she will listen and respond to emotions when handling the most sensitive and challenging of situations. This is a very unique ability, which would be such a positive asset as a parent. Morgan has always been sensitive to others needs and feelings and she has such a positive outlook on life that I know she would be a wonderful mother.

I've known Daniel for significantly less time (three years), but in that time I have come to know him as a very compassionate and sincere person. Daniel is such a welcome addition to our family. He has such a gentle nature that I know he would be an incredible parent.

Individually they are amazing people but together, they are a solid, loving couple who have vast amounts of love to share. The emotional environment in their home is a warm, safe place that any child would flourish in. Their lack of parental experience doesn't diminish the passion and love that they have for children.

I would not hesitate to charge Morgan and Daniel with the care of that which I hold the most dear in my life, my children.

I know first hand that parenthood is an adjustment even under the most ideal situations but I know that Morgan and Daniel are ready for this challenge and, I believe, they would be the best thing to happen to any child. They are ready for the challenges that parenthood brings and have tremendous amounts of love to share with someone. Please don't deny a child this life.

Daniel's sister wrote the following:

To Whom It May Concern:

This letter is in reference to Daniel and Morgan and their pending adoption application.

Over the course of my life I have had many ups and downs and had to rely heavily on family support to get through it, especially in the earlier years Daniel, and later on Daniel and Morgan. I was diagnosed with Thyroid cancer in 1998 and at that time I had a one year old daughter. Daniel was only in his first year of University then but he made time to travel off Island with me to medical appointments and was a great help in looking after my daughter. It was very hard to deal with treatments, surgery and medications with a child and very little help from my husband at that time, but luckily with help from my family, including Daniel, I got through it. Stress levels were high but his calm and collective manner kept us all in focus of what was important and our goal ahead.

In 2006 I found myself alone, separated, with three children and temporarily out of work. Who did I have to turn to? My family and this time that included Morgan. The first two people on my doorstep to offer help were Daniel and Morgan. I was a total disaster but they were there to listen, support and were never judgemental. When I met my current husband and remarried in 2008 they were both there again to support both of us.

Again in 2009 I was diagnosed with cancer, this time it was Cartoid Meningiomas. At this point our children were old enough to understand that I was sick, they knew what cancer was and they were terrified. Our eight year old developed her own medical issues (hyperglycemia) due to the stress. Daniel and Morgan took the girls under their wing. They cared for them, they listened to them, they took the time to explain everything to them, they let the girls cry on their shoulders. They let the girls be children, they allowed them to express themselves with no exceptions as to how the children should be reacting but instead took it one step at a time and worked with each girl individually. They were truly remarkable with the girls and I believe that their help and support, even in a time where they were feeling stress themselves because of my illness, is what got our girls through my tests and surgery.

Daniel and Morgan have a very strong bond with the girls. The girls spend a tremendous amount of time at their house. Whether it is doing crafts or baking with Morgan, playing games or just watching TV with Daniel, the girls love being there. We have travelled as a family with Daniel and Morgan and most of their time was on rides with the girls, walking around the zoo with the girls and I must admit, their patience is remarkable. We are so comfortable with the parenting skills and abilities that Daniel and Morgan have that we have listed them as guardians in our wills should we pass away before the girls are grown. Any child that would have an opportunity to have such loving, caring, and supportive parents would be truly blessed.

As I mentioned in the opening of this letter, there has been a tremendous amount of stress in our family over the years and Daniel, as well as Morgan now, have been a rock. The combination of their unique life experiences, their education and training as well as spending so much time with our children has given them the foundation that is needed to be wonderful parents. They are able to provide a structured environment where a child is allowed to be an individual and progress as an individual. No high or unrealistic expectations but rather unconditional love and support to help guide and nurture a child to the best that they can possibly be. Having been with our children over the past thirteen years, they have realized that having children includes many ups and downs but the joys of having your own child and being there and supporting them throughout those difficult times out weighs the negative. They are two very strong and capable individuals that together make a solid foundation for parents to a very lucky little person.

In closing, Morgan and Daniel, have the full support of my husband and I, and our children for this adoption. We will help and support them and their new son or daughter in any way we can. We both truly hope that you will approve the adoption application for Daniel and Morgan as they would be a wonderful blessing to any child. Please feel free to contact us at any time if you have any questions or need further clarification.

Thank you.

Our sisters were both truly supportive of us. They had known we had applied to adopt a child. They had been excited for us during the whole process. They suffered through the long waits between appointments and meetings, and hung on our every word as we gave them a general idea of where things were heading. Our sisters, along with our parents, had been shocked by our denied application.

They were aware that there was a lot of information they did not know, but they were all adamant that despite the unknowns we would be qualified and capable. They didn't know about the little boy specifically. They didn't know his history or his vast needs. But in their minds that didn't matter. They knew us. They knew what we had to offer. They were beyond positive that we could offer any child the life he or she would need to be successful in life. Daniel and I agreed.

Daniel and I knew the little boy. We knew his history and we knew the many needs and challenges that he would experience throughout his life. We knew and we were ready and willing to tackle any obstacles head on.

Not only did we know about the little boy. We had grown closer to him over the time span of the process. We had each spent a handful of times with the Kindergarten classes. Daniel with his shared reading, and me with computer activities. The little boy, like his peers, had grown close to us. They loved spending time with us and often initiated their own interactions with us when passing in the hallway.

The little boy too. Although he was very shy and withdrawn, he had begun to initiate interactions with us as well.

I had taken both Kindergarten classes to the computer lab several times. I was very careful not to pay any extra attention to the little boy. The lady had used the word "grooming". I had been molested as a child. "Grooming" was a dirty word. It made me feel uneasy. Neither Daniel nor I had any intentions of grooming the little boy, however we were not going to avoid the Kindergarten classes all together. We were both professional. We were able to continue our interactions without engaging in actions that could be considered grooming.

I had taken them to the computer lab the day before and was checking in with the teachers to see what they would like for their next visit to the lab. The children were all playing. Some of the children were playing with the puppet stage, others were playing with the over-sized doll house in the corner. Some were building things out of legos and blocks, and others were crawling around the floor dramatizing a dinosaur battle.

The little boy had been in the center of the room. He was building a gun out of brightly colored connecting blocks. He and another little boy were playing cops and robbers. The second little boy noticed me with his teachers and called out a cheery hello. The little boy looked up. I said hello to the boys and called out a hello to all the children. The little boy grinned and tipped his head down. He raised his colorful gun at me and very quietly told me to "stick em up." As I finished my conversation with the Kindergarten teachers I began to back away, playing along with the little boy and his friend. I held up my make believe shield and creatively dodged bullets as I danced my way out of the room.

This became routine for the little boy. Each time he saw me he grinned and shot me quickly and quietly with his finger. I would smile back at him. Many of the boys and girls began to look forward to these interactions and eventually I would be greeted by a room full of little fingers and brilliant smiles. Some of the girls were too delicate for shooting fingers. They chose instead to blow kisses, sending protective shields in my direction.

Daniel had similar experiences with the Kindergarten children. He too fell prey to little fingers and blown kisses. Regardless of the ammo, each was accompanied by big bright smiles. The little boy eventually began to speak in slightly more than a whisper. His voice was low, but no longer airy.

His trust and comfort with us continued to grow during the year. By the time Kindergarten ended, the little boy would speak to us in his regular voice. This was not the case for everyone and was only the case when there were no unfamiliar people around. Because we didn't spend a whole lot of time with the Kindergarten students, we had each only heard his regular voice once or twice.

We would love to ask the Kindergarten teachers for their support but we couldn't. We knew there was a possibility they would put one and two together and we could not risk violating the little boy's privacy or the confidentiality we had sworn to.

The first time they brought it up had been very painful. The Kindergarten teachers had brought up the adoption of the little boy several times. They were just trying to help. I knew that. They expressed a desire for someone in the community to adopt the little boy. They had seen so much progress in him. They wanted him to continue with his peer group. They expressed concerns for what would happen if he was relocated. Would he regress?

It was difficult to consider such things. Daniel and I didn't want to see the little boy regress. We wanted him to blossom. It was hard to be a casual participant in such conversations. I would just smile and nod. Safe reactions. I would try to give generic statements of optimism. Statements that could easily suggest an impartiality regarding the conversation and the little boy.

Instead of seeking the support of the Kindergarten teachers, Daniel and I approached another staff member. She knew Daniel and I both and would be able to provide a realistic and unbiased depiction of us. She was thrilled to hear that we were hoping to adopt a child. We didn't go into detail about being turned down. We just asked if she would be comfortable writing a letter on our behalf.

She didn't hesitate. She wrote the following, in hand-written cursive, wanting the most personal touch she could muster:

To Whom It May Concern

I am writing this letter to tell you about Daniel and Morgan and the many positive character traits which demonstrate that they would be wonderful parents!

Morgan and Daniel stand up for the rights of children while expecting, as every good parent should, that each child fulfill their own duty to become and be caring, thoughtful and responsible people. Individually, both Daniel and Morgan possess these positive parenting skills. As a couple, their common belief system makes them a strong parenting team!

Both as teachers and individuals, Daniel and Morgan demonstrate a strong natural understanding and empathy toward all children, which impresses everyone! I have had the privilege to know and work with both Morgan and Daniel for several years and daily I observe children benefiting from their strong convictions that children must be both respected and shown guidance! Morgan has helped troubled and insecure children make steps toward being positive, productive individuals. These girls and boys are given opportunities while being shown that someone cares about and respects them! I have seen Daniel deal with the frequent "emergencies" of children with the kindness and patience parents hope for in a teacher and strive to achieve themselves!

When I think of Daniel and Morgan the words nurturing, perceptive and competent come easily to mind. They show these traits daily in their personal and professional lives! They also have a strong support system, if needed, in their families, friends and church community. In short, they are naturals to be placed in the important role of parents! Anyone who has seen Morgan and Daniel interact with children knows this to be true! I am confident that they would completely and positively fulfill this most responsible and treasured opportunity of being a parent! Any child who is given the gift of Daniel and Morgan as parents will be truly blessed! If there is anything further which I can do to help reach a positive outcome, please call me anytime. Thank you for the opportunity to tell you about this amazing couple!

Sincerely

11 exclamation points. We were stunned by her amazing words, and the strength in her convictions. Despite our many thanks, she will never truly understand how thankful we really were. Regardless of the end result, her support had touched our hearts.

I was exceptionally close with My Aunt. She was honored to be able to support Daniel and me. She wrote amazing things as well. She poured her heart into her letter. Her letter was as follows:

To Whom It May Concern,

I am Morgan's aunt and have known her intimately since her birth. Morgan has been a very special person in her ability to keep me honest in my daily life. She is one of the most loving, giving, sharing, honest, caring, kind, compassionate women that I know. Even as a precocious toddler and child, she had the ability to express herself in the most direct and honest way. She meets all challenges in life whether it be personal or professional with the utmost bravery, focus, and intuitiveness. I admire her god given gifts of artistic creativity, empathetic listening, and unbridled passion for all she undertakes in life. Her family has always been first and foremost since her childhood years and then as a teacher her students. Ultimately her goal along with her husband is to have, love and raise their own family.

She is fiercely passionate, and loyal to those whom she loves and demands that we be thoughtful, honest and affectionate in expressing our own feelings. Morgan is a brilliant scholar, exceptional teacher and gifted debater. She is immensely dedicated to her family, students, friends and community. Her selfless-ness has always been evident to me by her uncanny ability to bring peace and healing in bro-kenness of spirit and community.

In each situation I have seen Morgan inter-act with children, be it my grand children, her nieces and nephews or strangers she always is the caring gentle teaching soul.

In closing I find it hard to express in words how utterly wonderful I believe it would be for any child to have Morgan as their beloved mother.

She phoned us immediately. She wanted us to know she was praying for us. We cried together. Everyone invested instantly in our potential family. Prayers were certainly a welcomed addition to our continued fight.

Our friend invested instantly as well. She was overjoyed to learn that she may be able to help us with our endeavor. She immediately wrote the following:

To whom it may concern

I have known both Daniel and Morgan on a personal as well as professional level for a number of years. I first met Daniel as a student teacher during his practice teaching at the school where I was a classroom teacher. I met Morgan a number of years later when taking an Assessment course through a local University. We were both working as Resource/Special Education teachers at different schools within the same school board. This was at a time before Morgan and Daniel were acquainted with each other. In the years to follow as fate would have it, they began teaching on the same staff. During this time I had the privilege of watching a wonderful work relationship develop between these two people, which blossomed into a beautiful friendship and then united into a solid marriage.

In has been wonderful to watch them grow together as a couple and support each other both in their personal goals and their professional endeavors. I was thrilled to hear of their desire to adopt a child. I couldn't think of a couple with more patience and love to give a child. With their exceptional personal qualities, strong family support, connection to the community, educational training, and work experience with children, they would make amazing parents to any child.

Speaking from experience of the teaching profession, we encounter children of very diverse backgrounds. I know Morgan and Daniel have extensive experience with children who come from the best of homes as well as children who have extremely difficult home situations. They have provided counsel, guidance, and support to young children who have been neglected, abused, have extreme emotional and/or social problems, learning disabilities, as well as psychological disorders. They are very skilled to handle any situation where children are concerned and they are very well liked and respected by the children they work with. They provide a sense of safety and security for the children they encounter on a daily basis and they have a great understanding of children in crisis. Morgan and Daniel have a love for children and the insight that most new parents don't have and it is for this reason I am certain they would be exceptional parents. Any child would be fortunate to have two people as nurturing and compassionate as they are to share in their lives with.

As a testament to the strength of Morgan and Daniel's relationship, they have shown great ability to juggle the stresses of their profession, as well as their personal and family life. They have had to cope with the serious illness of a sibling, the death of loved ones, the stressors of aging parents and of everyday life. They always impress me with their ability to see the realities in life whether good or bad and find the positive in it. Being a parent myself, this is valuable quality to have when raising children.

In closing, I would like to impress upon you that Morgan and Daniel are two very loving people who would provide a wonderful home life to a child. They are financially secure, they have the ability to deal with problems in a very positive way, they have experience with children of all ages, and most of all they have the desire to bring a child into their home to share their hearts with and make their family complete. It is my hope that you will consider them as adoptive parents.

Sincerely

She had attached her letter to an e-mail. She asked us to let her know if her letter was okay or if there were any changes we needed. Okay? Her letter was amazing! Her words were both kind and compassionate.

Daniel and I were truly loved and supported by our family and friends.

Next it was our turn. Daniel and I needed to write a letter on our own behalf. We needed to express ourselves. We needed to show the head lady who we were. For whatever reasons, who we were was not evident to the man and the woman who had assessed us, the man and woman who had rejected our application. We needed to rectify the situation.

Our letter was lengthy. It had to be. Not only did we need to express a true depiction of ourselves, we also needed to counter the reasons for which we had been declined. We needed to prove that we would be a match for the little boy.

Our letter stated the following:

Dear Head Lady,

It is difficult to get to know someone in a meaningful capacity in anything less than a lifetime; although many of us are forced to do so on a daily basis. Recently the man and the woman were introduced into our lives to make a determination regarding qualifications in the adoption of the little boy. The man and the woman were faced with the task of evaluating Daniel and I as individuals, as a couple, and as potential parents specifically for the little boy.

In the short amount of time we spent with the man and the woman, they were able to conduct and compile a home study, exploring our up-bringings, our family compositions and histories, as well gain an understanding of the qualities Daniel and I possess as people and would pass on to any child/children we might someday have in our lives.

Analyzing information is never an easy task, and we understand given the sensitivity and gravity of these life altering decisions, that this is not a task which is taken lightly. Despite the best efforts of everyone involved, information is generally analyzed in one of two ways: considering the best case scenario, or considering the worst case scenario. We realize that decisions which determine the fate of a child cannot be made under an unrealistic hope for the best case scenario, but must be made with the consideration for worst case scenarios as it is these worst case scenarios that sometimes result in the break-down of an adoption.

Having said this, Daniel and I would like the opportunity to share with you our interpretation of the facts which have led to the decision that we were not successful candidates for the adoption of the little boy. We have also included for your consideration, letters from people who have an intimate knowledge of Daniel and I individually and as a couple - letters which will provide a deeper and more intimate knowledge of Daniel and I than is possible to obtain in less than a handful of meetings. Although these letters are testimonials to our capacity as future parents, please be assured that we have shared no confidential information pertaining specifically to the little boy. We appreciate the time that has already been spent on our consideration but respectfully request this decision be reconsidered.

The man and the woman share a concern that Daniel and I are a young couple with no parental experience and high expectations. It is true that Daniel and I are a young couple, married only 2+ years, however our relationship extends beyond our two years of marriage as we have been best friends and colleagues for years prior to our marriage. Daniel and I share a passion for teaching as well as a love for children - children of all backgrounds and abilities. Although we have not yet had the privilege of working with the little boy directly, we are aware of the many needs the little boy has, and will continue to have throughout his life, and we are both willing and able to support such a child and to provide a safe and nurturing environment necessary for him to grow and develop as an individual.

We realize that a life with the little boy will not be an easy life. He will face many obstacles in his years to come: obstacles associated with

FASD; potential learning difficulties; social and emotional challenges related to abuse, neglect and loss; deep and complex connections with his biological family, cultural identity issues; difficulty establishing trusting relationships. This list is by no means exhaustive, but whatever the difficulty, Daniel and I would be there to support the little boy as he worked through these issues in his own way, and at his own pace.

Through the years, both as teachers and members of a larger community, Daniel and I have built a vast network of supports and resources which would benefit the little boy as an individual, Daniel and I as parents of a special needs child, and all of us as a family unit. These connections include advocacy groups, support groups, counsellors, specialists, as well as family members and friends.

One of the strongest supports we foresee for our family would be that of a friend and former colleague who raised three First Nations children as a single mother. Having been married to a First Nations man herself, she has status as a First Nations person and has an intimate understanding of both the culture, as well as the implications of raising First Nations children in a predominately Caucasian culture. She is also a guidance counsellor who understands the many complex issues faced by children and families.

She has counselled many children and families over the years and is by far one of the greatest supports our community has ever had. Our family would be blessed to have her support during the trying times we would surely experience as we grew together as a family.

Although Daniel and I do not have children of our own, we have worked with children of all magnitudes and have nurtured and supported each as they reached their own individual potential. Working in a school setting has given Daniel and I a deep understanding of children and of the things they need to be successful. Every child has the ability to achieve and the right to be successful members of his/her community - whether that community be school, home or the broader community in which he/she lives. This is not an unrealistic expectation but merely a fact of life. Every child has an individual capacity to grow, to learn, to achieve and to be successful.

The little boy has become a productive and successful member of the Kindergarten in his community. He has established positive friendships and has become relaxed in this environment. Daniel and I both work with the Kindergarten staff and students throughout the year – Daniel through literacy initiatives and myself as the school's technology contact. During the year we have watched the little boy grow and develop into a child who is able to verbally express himself, to laugh with friends, and to initiate interactions with the adults he is familiar with. Daniel and I would be able to offer the little boy a home in this community, where he would be able to continue going to school with his peers in an environment that has become safe and comfortable to him.

Throughout the year the Kindergarten class has explored their likes and dislikes, as well as their interests. We have come to learn that the little boy loves animals (particularly horses) and that he is involved in music lessons and has an affinity for drawing. The little boy enjoys playing soccer and has also expressed an interest in someday being able to play hockey. These are all dreams that Daniel and I would strive to make real for the little boy if chosen as appropriate parents for him. Being a young couple we may not have years of parenting experience, but we have the drive and energy level necessary to support an active child into their teen years and beyond. We have the drive, the energy level and the youth necessary to support the little boy as he continues into adulthood.

Despite what looks to the man and the woman to be a stress free and predictable life style, Daniel and I have experienced more than our fair share of stress in our few short years of marriage. We have experienced the losses of grandparents, the anxiety and emotional upheaval of terminal illnesses in our family, severe financial and emotional struggles of family members, as well as the daily stresses involved in being teachers. Through our work we have witnessed family violence situations, family break-downs, and the supports and resources necessary to support families and children in these situations. We have lived through the hurt our students experience, the hopelessness and helplessness many feel from day-to-day, and have been a voice of reason, compassionate listeners, strong shoulders and even sounding boards for students during times of exceptional crises.

Although our home life is currently significantly less stressful than we have experienced in the past, and our evening rituals can seem quite routine and predictable...this is only indicative of the day in which it happens. Each day presents its own set of challenges and each evening is a reflection of the day's experiences. Some nights we watch tv, some nights we go for a walk, some nights we sit around a fire pit and other nights we talk and deliberate serious issues until the wee hours of the night. Some nights we spend with extended family, some nights we host games nights, some nights we work on separate hobbies and other nights we are wakened in the wee hours of the morning by medical issues presenting in our animals and we bundle up and head out to access the emergency services provided by our local veterinarian's clinic. No two nights look the same. Life with a child would certainly be very different than the life we have experienced to date, however we welcome the trials and tribulations that would come with being the little boy's parents.

A lot of the questions we asked the man and the woman focused on the little boy's biological family and the relationship he has with them. We asked questions about the nature and characteristics of the little boy's siblings as it was disclosed that he has a strong and ongoing bond with his siblings. Although such questions could easily present as being representative of uneasiness, uncertainty, fearfulness, worry or even a need to control a situation, these questions are merely demonstrative of our belief that it is essential to gain as full an understanding as possible of all the dynamics in the little boy's life in order to provide him with the most stable environment possible. We realize that there will be many, many situations arise that we had never considered, and we are prepared to face them as we go, working through them as a family and tapping into our extensive support network when needed.

We are willing to foster the little boy's relationship with his siblings, knowing that they will not in turn foster his relationship with us and that they will attempt to undermine our family bond. We would be lying if we said this doesn't bother us. It does. We feel very badly about this as it will make it more difficult for the little boy to establish and maintain a strong bond with his forever family, regardless of who adopts him. This hostility which his siblings could/would present is discouraging, but it is by no means decision altering on our part. Given all of the little boy's issues, familial dynamics included, Daniel and I still believe we have the strengths, abilities and support system necessary to provide the little boy with a stable, loving and nurturing environment, and we are still willing and wanting to be parents to the little boy.

As previously mentioned, Daniel and I do not have any children of our own. It has recently been brought to light that the little boy would like to have siblings. The man and the woman said they would like to see the little boy's adoptive family replicate his biological family, possibly with parents in their late 40's who have children in their late teens, or who have previously parented children no longer in the home. Once again

I would like to reiterate that Daniel and I feel our youth would be an asset to the little boy, not only now, but in years to come.

As far as the little boy's desire to have siblings in his adoptive family, as of right now we can only guarantee him a dog who would love him to death, and five cats who would love to play with him during the day and curl up with him at night. Although these are not human siblings, much research has promoted relationships with animals as being therapeutic to children with emotional stresses and anxiety.

Daniel also has nieces who reside across the road from us. Daniel's sister has raised these girls as a single-mother for most of their lives and they have come to see Daniel as much more than just an uncle. He has a relationship with his family, particularly his nieces, which extends well beyond the boundaries of "extended family" and often resembles a relationship closer to that of father and daughters. The girls have looked up to Daniel their whole lives and are a daily constant in our lives. Given the opportunity, these girls would become as integral a part of the little boy's life as they are of ours. The youngest of the girls is the little boy's age and will, like the little boy, be entering grade one in the fall. She is an active and enthusiastic child who loves to play outside and who enjoys playing with children her own age. I believe that she and her sisters would be like family to the little boy and would become his "extended siblings" – if such a phrase exists.

As is noted in our file, Daniel and I are Caucasian and we are not overly educated in the Aboriginal culture. We do however have some education and experience worth mentioning. During my time at an Alternate School, a large percentage of our school's population were of Aboriginal descent – some of direct descent and others generations before. Being as the Alternate School's mandate was to meet the needs of the students on an individual basis (as opposed to a generic educational structure) we explored Aboriginal history with the school.

I taught a Mi'kmaq studies class in which we explored the historical time-line of the Mi'kmaq people and the effects of the Caucasian influence. As a school we had weekly sessions with a Shaman where we meditated, experienced mind journeys and explored our spiritual animals. We began and ended each session with the burning and smudging of sweet grass which holds significance in cleansing rituals associated with the Mi'kmaq culture. We examined and studied the medicine wheel and explored various Mi'kmaq artisans. We learned about and participated in creating porcupine quill art, dream catchers, and studied the poetry of Rita Joe. We had guest speakers in who talked about the hardships and racism they faced as Mi'kmaq peoples and many of our students shared their own stories of abuse and discrimination. We took our students on a field trip to a provincial park known for its natural beauty as well as its legendary connection to Gloosecap.

Although this education and experience does not constitute first-hand experiences with Mi'kmaq culture, I did spend a year of my life teaching in the arctic where I became painfully aware of the loss experienced by a people who are losing both their language and their culture. Similarly, Daniel has lived his whole life in our community and has been in the school system with many Mi'kmaq students who have struggled to meet the expectations of a culture not their own. Although the little boy is not currently living within his own culture, we do want to offer him every opportunity to experience his culture and to come to know and understand his identity as a Mi'kmaq.

Adopting the little boy involves many complex and dynamic issues. Daniel and I are willing to open our homes and our hearts to the little boy and to all that his life would involve. We are qualified and capable of providing the support, love and stability he will need.

Please consider not only our own testimony, but those of our family members and friends as evidence of our ability to be parents to the little boy. Thank you in advance for taking the time to readdress this issue and to consider our request with an open mind.

Sincerely

We really were sincere. As angry as we were at the way things had turned out so far, we were sincere. The thoughts, feelings, and opinions we expressed were sincere. We hoped our sincerity was obvious. Asking someone to change their mind was not always easy. Let me re-phrase that. The asking part was easy enough. *Convincing* someone to change their mind was the hard part.

CHAPTER 5

THE VISIT

WE HAD DONE ALL WE could. We had gathered our reinforcements and now it was time to suit up. We had called the head lady on our lunch break to inquire about submitting letters for her consideration. She sounded somewhat reluctant on the phone. It's a good thing Daniel and I weren't easily dissuaded.

It was the first day of our spring break. We arranged our reinforcements neatly into a light colored file folder and headed out. The weather was beautiful. It would have been a wonderful day to do something adventurous like many other teachers were doing. We had other things on our mind. We were shaping our destiny. That's big. A lot of pressure.

We were up bright and early. We triple checked everything. We might only have one shot at this. We wanted to make sure we'd have everything we'd need.

We arrived at the office of the head lady shortly after 11:00. Another maze. We were directed past several other department receptionists and up a small stairway. Three or four steps tops. We checked in with the receptionist at the bottom of the stairs. She was young. Probably in her late 20s. There was a young child with her. Probably her daughter. We were uncomfortable stating our business in front of the young girl. No guarantees of confidentiality with someone who is not an employee. Deep breath.

The receptionist took our information as the young girl watched curiously from her perch in the back of the very tiny office. The receptionist was neither friendly nor non-friendly. She was indifferent. Of course she was. Why wouldn't she be? What did it matter to her?

"Does she know you're here?" She was referring to the head lady. I had told the head lady on Friday that we'd be dropping off the letters sometime this week. She motioned up the three or four stairs through the plexiglass window. "Wait up there."

We climbed the stairs and turned into the little waiting area. It was quaint. There were fake plants in several of the corners – trying to accomplish a more homey feel. There was a large painting on the only full wall in the waiting area. It was abstract. It was kind of womb-like. It made Daniel feel awkward. I giggled. I hadn't giggled in a long time. It felt nice to be relaxed, even if for just a few seconds.

People walked past the little waiting room, going here and there. We tried to guess which, if any of the women, might have been the head lady.

Many minutes had passed – maybe close to twenty. We heard the receptionist on the phone. We heard her say "yes they're still here. I know it's almost lunch." It was later than we thought. Over thirty minutes had passed. We wondered if she meant us. We were the only ones in the waiting room. We wondered if they were hoping to wait us out. Hoping we would get discouraged waiting and would just leave. Did they not know what was at stake for us? We'd have camped out overnight had we needed to. We were committed to the little boy and to our future family.

A young woman entered the waiting room. She seemed frazzled. She was dressed up. She had high-heels on and a three-quarter length dress coat. Her hair was clipped neatly at the back of her head and her long bangs fell on either side of her face. I wondered why she was there. Was she hoping to adopt? Was she being investigated?

She waited a few minutes and then checked in with the receptionist. The receptionist asked if she had an appointment. She said she had had an appointment on Friday but was unable to make it so had rescheduled for today. The receptionist didn't sound impressed. She made a few calls to see if anyone was expecting the young woman.

The young woman returned to the waiting room. She sat across from the large abstract womb. She fidgeted with her coat and her pantyhose. Probably nervous. She took a cell phone out of her small purse and checked her phone messages. She took notes as the messages played over speaker phone. Nothing overly interesting. She fiddled with her pen and paper, putting them back into her purse when she was finished listening to her messages. She had saved some and deleted others. She looked around and checked her watch. She had checked it several times already. I wondered if she was on a lunch break. She eventually left. No one had come to get her and I assumed she couldn't wait any longer.

Daniel and I were alone again. Waiting. We had been doing a lot of that lately. We were getting good at it. I had grown used to re-living fond memories. Today though I had no need to live in happy memories. Daniel and I were not as nervous as we had been. The worst was over. We had already been told no. Things could only get better.

More people passed by. In and out. In and out. Some to and from a stairwell, others to and from a door adjacent to the stairwell. Both required security cards. The stairwell didn't intrigue me. I was intrigued by the other door. I wondered where it went. I wondered what the need was for such security. I wondered what would happen if I followed someone through the door. Were there security guards? Would an alarm sound? Would someone come running after me?

I caught Daniel frowning up at the big womb again. I giggled again. "At least it's colorful," I offered. "Do you think she's going to come?" I asked him. He checked his watch again. 11:50 am. Almost lunch. Perhaps they would wait until after lunch. See how dedicated we were.

Daniel and I had often questioned whether an initial rejection was part of the process. A way to determine whether or not people would advocate for their future children. That's not why we were pursuing things. I actually hoped this was not some part of the process. I thought it was cruel. I didn't want to believe something so cruel would be intentional. Either way - we were advocating.

A chubby, artificially blonde lady appeared in the doorway. She had emerged from the short staircase outside the receptionist's office. Interesting. I had expected her to be behind the security protected doors. She extended her hand while at the same time letting us know she could only spare us five minutes. She also made reference to not having realized she was to be expecting us. Daniel was quick to reply that we had told her we'd be bringing our letters once we had accumulated them.

We followed her to her office. Down the little staircase, past the receptionist's office, past the other department receptionists and out the main door. We crossed the busy hallway into a separate group of offices. She worked out of here. Interesting. No signs or labels to direct people to this side of the building. Must not like being disturbed.

She motioned us to sit down. We took the two chairs immediately inside her office. Her office was longer than it was wide. She had a desk and computer at the back of the office, in front of the only window in the room. We were seated at a small round table in front of her work area. She smiled as she sat down. Her smile seemed patronizing. I wasn't sure. Perhaps I was just being skeptical. Be open-minded.

Daniel began. He told her about our letters - ours and those of our family and friends. She cut him off. She smiled again. Patronizing? She heard the disappointment in my voice, she told us. When we had called her Friday from work. She had heard the disappointment in my voice. Interesting. I had not been disappointed when I spoke to her. I was polite and professional, knowing that would be the best avenue to have her reconsider the decision.

The fact that she would even know my voice well enough to identify how I was feeling seemed unrealistic to me. I had only spoken to her once before. Well before Christmas. Requesting the application form and clarifying what process Daniel and I would need to pursue for a child-specific adoption. And yet Friday, months later, she was able to detect an emotion in my voice that hadn't even been there. Interesting. Patronizing?

"EAP," she continued. EAP. I didn't know what that was. I wondered if Daniel knew what that was. Was that the appropriate appeal process? "Counselling?" Daniel asked confused. "Yes," she smiled again. Patronizing. Lovely. Here we go again. "No," Daniel stated. Things were not going as planned. Redirect. Back to our reinforcements. "We have testimonials from people who know Daniel and I very well," I began. "We would like for you to read them. We are hoping they may provide enough insight into the situation that you would consider reviewing the decision." Strong. Matter of fact. No emotions to misinterpret.

Daniel offered her our file. She patted it, smiling again. Patted it. "Well," she began, "I haven't seen the official report yet, and I'll be going on vacation before the official report is finalized. I will be gone until the end of April. I could read them when I get back if you want." If we want? Of course we wanted. Wasn't that the point of this meeting?

Finalized. The word was stuck in my head. The report isn't finalized. I inquired. The head lady explained that the man and woman had documented our reactions during our last meeting. They had recorded our reactions to the rejection and were adding them to our report - to our file.

Anger. Stay quiet. Just listen.

She looked at her watch and began to stand up. Our time was up. She had given us the five minutes she had promised and was not interested in giving us a minute more. It was lunch time. She was leaving.

Yes. Yes we wanted her to look at our file when she returned.

Daniel and I remained quiet as we left her office and left the building. We got into our vehicle. Daniel didn't start the engine right away. He sat back and gave a look of disbelieve at the outside of the window. "Yup," I said. I knew Daniel well. We were both thinking the same thing. We were completely and utterly shocked at how political the system was.

The head lady had made sure to include in our five minute time allotment, her full confidence in her staff and their ability to reach appropriate decisions. We pointed out that some adoptions break down. These instances, in our minds, represented decisions that had been made in error. We urged her to consider that our situation might be that of the opposite magnitude. The decision in our instance might be an error resulting in an appropriate placement not being made.

"Yup," Daniel agreed. "Nice," I said. Daniel knew I intended this to be sarcastic. It wasn't nice at all. It was terrible. Once a decision was made there was a whole CYA (cover your ass) philosophy of everyone involved. No one was going to admit to any flaws. That would look negatively on all of them. Theirs was a flawless system. Yes because that really exists on our side of the rainbow. I was not discouraged. I was angry. Daniel was too.

This only added fuel to our fire. We were now more determined than ever to find someone who would listen to us.

"Remember," she had said smiling. Again with that patronizing smile. "You matched yourself with him, not us." What the hell did that mean? We hadn't gone out soliciting children who were up for adoption and picked one at random. We had become aware of a child in our school in need of a forever home. We had not actively sought this situation. It had just happened. The match had presented itself.

We phoned our parents. They had known our plans for the day. They were hopeful. We recounted our visit - all five minutes of it - as best as we could. Although it had only transpired moments earlier, it was still hard to remember every detail of the conversation. We highlighted the main ideas - and the patronizing attitude.

People in positions of power dealing with situations of such a sensitive nature should be trained in people skills. Even if we were just grieving and in denial, as the head lady felt was the case, a little professional sincerity would have been nice. Although, in her defense, she had told us that the process was a clinical one and not a personal one. That was about two seconds before pointing out that their department was not responsible for matching us with the little boy; we were.

Sigh. We finished our calls and Daniel started the engine.

CHAPTER 6

THE NEXT STEP

I FELT BAD FOR DANIEL. This was an emotional roller coaster. Daniel was not the type of person to set his hopes on things that were unrealistic or unattainable. He did not like the disappointment. I didn't mind getting my hopes up. I enjoyed the excitement and looking forward to the things that accompany high hopes.

I hated dragging him through this. I knew it was something we were both striving for, but I also knew he needed time to digest everything before plunging ahead. I was ready for the plunge. I needed to assess where he was with everything.

We went out to eat. Although the situation was preoccupying both our minds, it was not always a welcomed topic of conversation. I tiptoed around the topic. Treading gently. I knew this was a lot for Daniel. We had both dreamed of having children. We had shared that dream forever. Daniel would consider today to be a major set-back. We had had so many hopes for how today was going to go. This would definitely qualify as a disappointment.

"There's gotta be someone other than her," he had said. I nearly fell off my chair. He just opened the conversation that way. So much for tiptoeing. I waited. Daniel was a deep person. He didn't just throw out statements or comments. He meant what he said. His comments were always connected to what he thought, knew, or believed. His remark would be followed through with a rationale. I waited.

"It's ridiculous," he continued. "It's not like we're asking them to just change their minds. We are asking them to review their decision." He took a bite of his meal. He was processing. I could see it in his eyes. "Who can we call?" he asked. I wasn't sure. There were several ways we could go about things.

There was still a possibility that the head lady would look at our file. That some form of professional obligation would at least require her to open the file and look at the letters. Whether or not she would do this with an open mind was another story.

So, we could either fight hard - burning all our bridges as we went, or continue to placate with people who may be willing to listen to us. Being as we were not sure where the head lady would eventually fall, we decided against burning any bridges just yet.

That meant there was no point in pursuing the legal route to access our file. We had asked her about it. Asked if we could have a copy of our file. We received an adamant no to that question. There was information about the boy in our file which we did not have a right to see. We requested a copy of our file with any and all information pertaining specifically to the little boy removed. Again a no. The file was the property of the organization. We would not receive a copy.

> *That had annoyed Daniel. "We have a right to see the information that pertains to us," he had told the head lady. She did not agree. According to her the only right we had was to request to have the file read to us. She then pointed out that we had turned down that offer previously. Me. That was my fault. I had nearly spat the words "no thank you," at the woman when she had offered. No point looking backwards. Forward thinking only.*

So, for the time being we would not enact the freedom of information act. We knew it had been done before. We knew it had been done before in a situation similar to ours. Precedent had been set. If we needed to, we would contact a lawyer later. We would obtain a copy of our file if, and when necessary. It wouldn't matter if names and other specifics were blacked out. We were not trying to obtain information about other people. We were not trying to access any information about the little boy or his family. We wanted to know what the man and woman had written about us. The specifics.

We drove back home. An hour and a half. I jotted down possible next steps as Daniel drove. He was surprisingly upbeat given the circumstances. He was entirely invested in changing the outcome of the decision from a month ago. I love Daniel.

I made a few calls on the cell phone. I gathered names and numbers. We had a few avenues. We didn't know if we should continue climbing up the ladder, or just start at the top and go for the gold. We figured starting at the top would step on a lot of toes. We knew that people didn't usually react kindly to having their toes stepped on.

This brought our thoughts back to the head lady. We needed to decide if we wanted to wait another month to see where things would go with her, or if we wanted to move forward. Moving forward would definitely step on her toes. Did we want to step on her toes? Would that come back to bite us in the behind? Time was such a precious commodity. Could we afford to waste another month?

He was so small and insecure. He was already six. That's old for a child waiting to be adopted. The older the children are the more difficult it is to find them a match. To find them a forever home. Most adoptive parents sign up for infants. For children who have not yet been damaged by unhealthy life experiences.

Not us. Not now. Maybe had we filled out an application before encountering the little boy.

But things had not worked out like that for us. We had encountered him first. He had touched our hearts instantly. He was our reason for adopting. It didn't matter that he was older. It didn't matter that his age and his life experiences had classified him as special needs by system standards.

We wanted the best for him. We were willing to admit that that might not mean us. We were okay with that so long as the decision was made fairly and was in his best interest. They always said they were in the business of finding homes for children - not finding children for homes. We were fine with that.

Our issue was that with every passing day the little boy was getting older. His age would work against him. He had already been disadvantaged by things outside of his control. I wanted good things for him. I wanted those good things to happen for him as quickly as they could.

Counselor. We considered enrolling in family counseling. Enrolling in courses or programming that would strengthen our skills as potential parents. That would all happen later according to system protocol. Support and programming are a later part of the process. Part of the process we had not successfully progressed to. So, counseling?

Would it benefit us to begin some parenting processes on our own? Would that be stepping on toes?

Would it just illustrate our willingness to accept support and identify and work on our weaknesses?

I should have said yes. When the lady had asked if we wanted to hear the whole report I should have said yes. That way we would have known what areas we had demonstrated weaknesses in and what areas we needed to concentrate on. Hind sight is 20/20. Forward looking only.

One choice to make. Wait or don't wait. Don't wait. Waiting would not benefit the little boy, regardless of the final decision. We knew this for a fact. It had been thrown at us.

> *"We don't begrudge him a happy home." Daniel had said that. He had said that to the woman when she was explaining why we would not be the little boy's parents. Daniel had said he would be content knowing they had found a match—a better match than us—for the little boy. That was when she had told him there was no successful match found. "So you'd rather him stay in a foster home forever than be with us?" Daniel had asked. "Yes," she answered coldly. Daniel expressed his disdain for their choice to potentially leave the little boy in foster home forever than to place him with us.*
>
> *She didn't like that. She didn't like Daniel questioning her decisions. She had shot back.*

She didn't just shoot to maim, she went straight for the jugular. "The time we spent considering your application was time that was taken away from finding a positive match for the little boy." She might as well have said "time that was needlessly taken away." Bitter. She was bitter and cold.

Compassionless. Absolutely no consideration for the broken dream in front of her. She didn't care. She had told us that early on. She was not here for us. She was here for the little boy. We were there for the little boy too.

We were not suggesting there was no better match for him than us. We were suggesting that our rejection should not have been based on the reasons provided. Those reasons were not accurate. They were not valid. They didn't make sense. The reasons seemed to exist because of the decision. That wasn't how it was supposed to work. The decision was supposed to exist because of the reasons, not the other way around. Something wasn't adding up.

She was 100% confident in her decision. That bothered me. Something didn't add up. How can anyone be 100% confident in something that doesn't add up? I hated her.

My heart bled for Daniel. She had gone for the jugular. It was our fault a match hadn't been made yet. We had taken up precious time.

> *We had taken time away from him - time that could have been spent finding his forever home.*

We would not make that mistake again. Don't wait. Move forward. We would not bother the minister of health just yet. We would call the lady above the head lady. We would call the top lady. We would call her and plead our case.

CHAPTER 7

OUR PLEA

DEEP BREATH. WE KNEW WE were nearing the end of the trail. If we did not soon find someone willing to listen, we would be out of options. We were nervous. Each step brought us closer to an end. I wanted Daniel to phone. Daniel wanted me to phone. We were both nervous. Daniel sometimes stutters when he is nervous. That bothers him.

Daniel didn't want to phone. He didn't want to stutter on the phone with the top lady. He didn't want to mess anything up. I love Daniel. His stutter was never as bad as he thought it was. I knew he wouldn't mess things up, but I knew he was uncomfortable. I would phone.

When I dialed the number I got a receptionist. The top lady was not in. Her receptionist would send her an e-mail. She would call us back. The top lady was quick to call back - same day. She inquired as to the nature of our call. We didn't want to have the conversation over the phone. We thought we would do better in person. We gave her a general overview.

She was a divisional top lady. There was another top lady who was director of the adoption department. The top lady would have her receptionist arrange a meeting with the two top ladies, Daniel, and me. The receptionist would get back to us with a date. We would have to wait until the beginning of the week as the top lady of adoption was currently away.

We waited. We were good at that now. We busied ourselves with other things. We delved even deeper into our work. Our stress was a definite benefit to our students.

The next week came and went. No call. Not a good sign. It was confusing. The top lady had seemed so on-the-ball. She had seemed eager to meet with us, willing to listen, and able to remain open minded. It was confusing. Still no call.

Back to the age-old dilemma. How soon is too soon to call back? We didn't want to look over-eager or impatient. We didn't want to risk looking disinterested if we let things go. Time was wasting. Sigh. We would call the receptionist.

Third ring. Cheerful hello. I inquired about the meeting. Silence. I provided more details and inquired again. Hesitation followed by a confused response. She knew nothing about the meeting. She had not been asked to arrange a meeting. She called back within five minutes with a date and time.

Daniel and I surmised reasons for the mix up. It was a little disappointing. The top lady had been so willing, so obliging. It was disappointing to think that she hadn't even attempted to arrange the meeting as promised. It was disappointing to think that she may not be as on-the-ball as we had originally thought. Not a good sign. No point getting stuck on the small stuff. Daniel and I had a meeting to plan for.

It was another long drive. Close to two hours. We had left school immediately following the bell. We arrived in the parking lot with ten minutes to spare. We parked at the far end of the parking lot. We wanted the brisk walk in the fresh air. We wanted to kill a few minutes. Didn't want to look over-eager. We arrived in the waiting area with five minutes to spare. We read the posters on the wall and the pamphlets in the display area. We talked jovially. We tried to keep ourselves distracted. No point psyching ourselves out.

I was getting nervous. It was past 4:00. Five minutes past to be exact. Deep breath. I wrapped my pinky around Daniel's. I didn't look up at him. I tried to keep myself focused. Calming breaths.

The office was busy. There were cubicles in every direction. People appeared and disappeared above the horizon of cubicles. People moved to and from various areas. Everyone seemed to be in a good mood. It had been a beautiful weekend. More hustle and bustle. We played the guessing game again, wondering which, if any, of the women was the top lady. We guessed the personality of the various women passing by.

Daniel had just finished checking his watch again. 4:10pm. A confident lady approached. She held out her hand and introduced herself. She was the top lady. She had a hand shake that could bring a grown man to his knees. Power. Power or confidence. It was hard to tell. I wondered if it was genuine confidence or an attitude she had to acquire in order to make it in an industry that had once been male dominated.

We followed her into the room. We sat. Daniel looked comfortable. I didn't take my jacket off. I was nervous. I felt comfortable in my jacket.

The top adoption lady stood and shook our hands. Her handshake wasn't painful. It was warm and friendly. They both sat. They were sitting directly across from Daniel and I. The table was huge. It took up the entire room. There was room for another twelve people around the table.

The divisional top lady spoke first. She wanted us to know she had not looked at our file. For a fleeting instance I wondered if that was a good thing or not. She continued to explain that neither of them had wanted to be biased. They wanted to meet with us. They wanted to meet with us and listen to our story without any previous bias.

We spent an hour with the two top ladies. We started at the beginning—the very beginning—going back to the first time we had become aware of the little boy. We walked them through our experiences from start to finish. They took some notes, interjected thoughts and opinions, and stopped to ask questions along the way. Our story seemed to come out in one long, much-needed breath. Exhale. It felt nice to be able to talk to someone - to be able to tell everything without having to sensor information for confidentiality reasons.

They were both very nice. They shared our every emotion as we told our story. We laughed together, we shared hurts and disappointments, and we shared frustrations. They expressed their own concerns over various aspects of our story.

They were concerned that our process had happened too quickly; that there hadn't been enough time to develop an appropriate relationship with our workers. They wondered about a personality conflict. I assumed they were referring to the woman. They didn't say.

The man had seemed okay. He had seemed to distance himself from the final decision during our last meeting with them. He had been assigned as the primary worker but he had not been the one to read the report to us. He had not been overly talkative during the meeting. He had not expressed any ownership over the decision. He had not been the one to state 100% confidence in the decision.

They wanted to look into our situation. Both ladies expressed admiration for Daniel and me. They admired our strength and determination. They admired our advocacy efforts. They thought it showed strength of character to advocate for ourselves. They were going to look at our file.

They were sure to be very clear that there were no guarantees. The decision might not be reversed. They again stressed their concern over the speed with which things were done. In their hour with us they did not see anything that would automatically rule us out as a possible match. They said so. They then cautioned us from assuming this meant things would change. They would look into it, bottom line.

That was all Daniel and I had been hoping for. We had wanted the opportunity to be listened to. We had wanted someone to look into our situation and make sure things had happened for all the right reasons. If there was even the smallest chance that a mistake had been made, we wanted to find someone willing to rectify it.

We had found those people. The top adoption lady would call us back. She would call back when the head lady - who was on vacation until the end of April - returned back. By then the report would be completed.

Daniel and I skipped out of the building and across the parking lot. We felt 1000 pounds lighter. We hadn't realized how much pressure we had been under. This was an entire relief. We knew and understood that we still might not end up parenting the little boy, but at least we were assured that the decision would be made fairly this time. No conflicts of interest. No influential relationships with the biological mother or siblings. Open, unbiased minds. We were happy.

We jumped into the vehicle and phoned our parents. That had become a regular routine for us. Our parents had been closely following the events pertaining to the adoption and were anxious for updates when they became available. A positive phone call. We couldn't remember the last time we'd gotten to make positive phone calls.

We hoped and dreamed all the way home. We talked about the "what if" and "imagine when" scenarios of a life with the little boy. For the first time in a long time we allowed ourselves to be unguardedly hopeful. We each said a silent prayer. We had been definitely blessed to have pursued the adoption past the initial "no" and to have found the two top ladies.

We wondered how many other potential parents might have been turned down for unfounded reasons. We wondered if they had appealed their decisions. We wondered if they had experienced success. Daniel and I had not necessarily experienced success, but we knew our situation would at least be dealt with fairly. That in itself was a success.

Back to the waiting. This time the waiting was not so bad. We had faith in the two top ladies. We had faith that things would turn out for the best. The days passed - some slower than others.

The end of April came and went. No call. Not necessarily a bad thing. How long might it take to access the final report? She and the head lady would have to meet. They would have to discuss everything. They would have our letters to read as well. They might want to meet with the man and woman who had assessed us. Those things could take a while. We would wait a while longer.

We waited. We decided to call in the second week of May if we had not heard back by then. May had started out to be a horrible month. Many schools in our district had experienced staffing cuts. Our school had been no different. We were down a handful of kids. We expected to lose part of a position. That was always stressful for everyone in the school.

Our school was cut two full positions. Shock and devastation rocked the school. Ranks had been jumped and situations manipulated. Daniel was one of the two staff to be relocated. The union was involved. The community rioted. Letters were sent to the school and the school board. Things were tense - to say the least.

The day we found out Daniel was being relocated, we decided to pursue some good news. We decided to call the adoption top lady. To inquire about how things were going. She didn't seem to know who I was at first. Not a good sign. This may not be the good news venue we were hoping for. Something hadn't happened yet - either she hadn't met the head lady or hadn't gotten the report - either way she would call back the following week.

The following week came and went. No call. Things were still bad at work. The union didn't feel confident in their ability to rectify anything. Things were not clear cut. It would be difficult to prove anything.

I wanted to call the adoption top lady again. Today would be a great day for some good news. We wouldn't hold our breath, but we would cross our fingers. That became a slogan for us. "We won't hold our breath, but we'll definitely cross our fingers." Better phone call this time. She apologized for not getting a hold of us the week before as promised. She had been out of province. She had been in contact with the head lady. They both agreed to have two new workers continue with our case. Again the reiteration that this was by no means a promise or guarantee of a different outcome. Just a way to rectify what she still felt might have been a personality conflict.

That was great news. We clung to the hope of two new workers looking into things. That was great. Again no promises. We knew the deal. We were hopeful nonetheless. We'd hear back from either her, or the head lady in the week to come.

That next week came and went. By this time we never expected to receive phone calls when promised. We began to use a three days grace rule. We called back three days after having expected their call. That seemed like a safe rule.

The next call was confusing. It didn't follow from our last call at all. She still hadn't read the file but believed that the original workers may have been aware of a red flag that only people working with us could identify - a testament to her confidence in those people working in the system.

That confused Daniel and I. Not that we were suggesting the original workers were incompetent. We had never felt that. We just felt their decisions were not based on solid, valid justifications.

The top adoption lady admitted to not knowing the little boy. I didn't understand why that mattered. I wasn't sure where the conversation was going. She had seen him though. She knew what he looked like. He was cute. I agree. He is cute. He is sweet and kind too. Suddenly the adoption top lady was talking about people often falling in love with cuteness and not with reality. Daniel and I were confused. Why the sudden change? She said she hadn't read the file. Where was this change in attitude coming from?

She hadn't read the file because it was being rewritten. That was odd. Why would it be rewritten? Daniel and I began to fear a CYA (cover your ass) conspiracy. Had our letters been used to revamp our file so that our standpoints were no longer valid? That was too hard to believe. Neither Daniel nor I wanted to believe that a system designed and developed to look after the best interest of children could be so corrupt. We were confused. The conversation left us floundering.

"What about the two new workers?" I asked. I was struggling to make any connection between my last phone call and this one. Had it not been for her voice I would have wondered if I was even talking to the same lady. "Oh yes." That's how she reassured me. She followed her "oh yes" by a big fat "if" that had never existed before. "If we proceed with things we will definitely assign two new workers to the case." If. Where did that come from?

I wanted to wake up. This could not be reality. This was one of those twilight zone moments again. I was beginning to think I was losing my mind. Daniel would be my measure. I recounted the conversation to Daniel. He had been driving and had not been able to listen to the conversation. I re-enacted the conversation as best as I could. I forced myself to be as emotionless as possible. I did not want Daniel to know how furious I was. I wanted to gauge his reaction. I wanted to see if I was overreacting or not.

Daniel would be the bar. He was neither overly optimistic nor overly pessimistic in life. He was usually realistic. He would provide a realistic reaction to the phone conversation. I looked at him. He looked confused. He asked who I had been talking to. I had already told him that. He had known who I was calling when I started the phone call. He was obviously - and from my perspective understandably - confused. "The top adoption lady," I responded matter-of-factly.

Daniel had me repeat the conversation again. It made me feel better that he was so confused. At least I knew I wasn't losing my mind. Daniel described the phone call as a complete 180. He mused as to why the change of heart. If she hadn't read the file, where had the new perspective come from? All we knew was that she had met with the head lady. Wow. Powerful head lady.

The adoption top lady promised to call the next day. 4:00 pm. We gave her our cell phone number - again. We wanted to ensure she would reach us no matter where we were. At 4:50 pm the following day she phoned our home phone. She had allegedly phoned our cell phone and got an "out of area" message. I glanced at the cell phone. It was on the table. It was turned on. It had been on all day. Battery level registered as high. Signal registered as strong - three bars. No missed calls were registered. Odd.

Neither Daniel or I have full faith in technology. Glitches happen all the time. It was possible she was telling the truth. We weren't going to wager a guess at this point in the game. Nothing was as it seemed. It didn't really matter either way. She was calling to tell us that she had not received our file - or had not received it in time to have read it yet - it was becoming hard to keep everything straight. It didn't really matter either way. The bottom line was the same. She would read it and get back to us. No date given this time. Again we would wait.

We had enough to keep us busy in the meantime. Daniel was completing a thesis and I was finishing up a course in educational leadership. Even without those distractions work would keep us distracted for weeks to come. Daniel had still not gotten anywhere with the union and parent protests were falling on deaf ears. Daniel would be going to a school similar in population to where we were now.

Daniel was not looking forward to the move. It had nothing to do with the school itself. He knew and respected the principal and the vice-principal. He also knew a few of the staff and had worked in that community during his teaching practicum. His issue was with the way things had been handled. Our lives were completely dictated by politics at the moment.

Staff members were angry. People were bitter. The way things are handled is usually more important than anything else. Things had been handled poorly. Our staff was split. There was a huge divide. Morale was at an all-time low. Things were not positive.

Daniel was not the only one to experience change. I applied for a job with the district. I could no longer tolerate working under such political manipulation. I accepted the job four hours after interviewing for it. Next year would mean changes for both Daniel and I. Things would be different. Things would be busy.

We wondered if we would add parenthood to our list of upcoming changes. We were still hopeful. Despite the multiple misunderstandings and confusions, we were still hopeful. We discussed the issue of paternity/maternity. As it stood, I had accepted the position of a specialist consultant with the district. I agreed to a minimum five year commitment. A lot of time and money would be invested into my training. I would not be able to take time off if we were chosen as a match for the little boy.

That would actually work out better all the way around. The little boy would benefit from a strong father-son bond. I would be able to continue my training. Daniel would be a stay-at-home Dad and would not have to move to a new school right away. Of course, this was assuming things worked out for our dream family. And this was also assuming things happened within the next few months. Judging by the way things had progressed to date, this was not very likely. But, it didn't hurt to dream.

On top of all of that, Daniel had enrolled in a PhD program for the upcoming school year. Much of the program could be completed online, however there was an on-campus requirement. This meant that Daniel would spend one day per week off Island.

Daniel and I spent our days dreaming about the upcoming year. We loved to fantasize about how wonderful it would be if things all worked out. If things were as such that the little boy and I could accompany Daniel off Island each week. Keeping the little boy up to date on his class work would not be a problem as Daniel and I were both educators. The trips themselves would provide amazing quality time and countless experiences we would cherish forever. We talked about where we would go out to eat and fun places we would visit on our way to or from the University.

As of right now it was just a dream. It was just sometimes nice to be able to dream - to think happy thoughts. My new job might even allow for those dreams. In my first year, I was expected to take an online program with a focus on applied behavior analysis. My weeks would be divided into three categories: I would shadow our department head three days each week, I would shadow our district representatives one day a week, and I would spend one day a week studying.

It would be possible to accompany Daniel on my study day if it fell on the same day as Daniel's program. We wondered if I would have any control over that. We had so many things going on in our lives, so much stress and political crap attempting to influence our moods, and yet we were happy and hopeful. No crap - no matter how severe - could possibly taint the joy we would experience if we were able to start a family. There were days when that was the only bright spot on the horizon.

We held on to that hope. We would easily sacrifice any and all of our many aspirations, for a family of our own. Daniel and I wanted to be parents more than we wanted any of the other things to which we were aspiring.

CHAPTER 8

MORE WAITING

IT WAS BECOMING INCREASINGLY DIFFICULT to keep track of things. When had we talked to anyone last? Who were we waiting to hear back from? It was never hard to remember we were waiting for a phone call - it was hard to remember: from who, for what, and where were we in the process.

Daniel and I had begun to keep a note pad. We wrote everything to date as best as we could from the first day we saw the little boy. To date we were waiting for another phone call from the adoption top lady. She was still waiting for the newest version of our file and would call us once she had read it.

I would never forgive myself for having turned down the opportunity to hear the original report read. Now we would never know what changes had been made. We could not argue the changes or even fully understand exactly how biased they may or may not have been.

Daniel had been fully supportive of my decision at the time. He knew my heart was broken and that I had wanted to escape the room before my emotions got the best of me. I love Daniel. He knows me better than anyone in the world. I will never forgive myself for not having been stronger at that moment. For not having been able to bury my emotions long enough to have listened to that report.

Forward looking only. We didn't hear back from the adoption top lady for weeks. We decided, like usual, to call her to inquire where we were in the process. At this point in time we knew her phone number off by heart.

I was heading to a half day in-service in the adoption top lady's municipality. I would call her on my break. It would be easier for me to call her than it would for Daniel. He'd be in classes all day and it was his duty day on top of that so he would have little free time. Not that it had mattered much in the end. There was no lengthy conversation that would have made him late for class. As a matter of fact, there was no conversation at all.

The lady who had answered the phone provided a name and position I had not heard before. She was definitely not who I was looking for. She was not the adoption top lady.

I apologized for the inconvenience and suggested I must have had the wrong number. The lady inquired as to who I was looking for and then confirmed that I did have the right number. The adoption top lady was on another call and so all incoming calls were redirected to a receptionist.

The receptionist would check to see if the adoption top lady was almost through with her phone call. If she was I could hold, otherwise she'd have the adoption top lady return my call. She asked for my name. I explained who I was, although in the back of my mind I assumed that would be the determining factor for whether or not the adoption top lady was available.

I was not at all surprised when the receptionist told me that the adoption top lady would return my call. I gave her my cell phone number and headed for home. There was a lot of construction on the roads and the drive took me just over two hours. Although I had half-expected a phone call from the adoption top lady, my phone did not ring for the rest of the day.

Daniel and I waited all evening for her to return our call. She had told us multiple times that she often is so busy she returns calls well into the evening. We waited all evening. We eventually gave up on the call and went to bed.

We glanced at the phone as soon as the alarm clock began to buzz. We both knew that was ridiculous. She would not have called us after 10 pm. But we glanced none-the-less. No new calls. We sighed as we got out of bed. Daniel jumped in the shower and I started breakfast.

I was beginning to feel as though my life had become a sequel to *Groundhog Day*. Our days all seemed to start and end the same way. Despite the frustrations we were experiencing we did our best to remain hopeful. We continued to dream and fantasize about our lives as one big happy family.

That is an unrealistic expectation the man had said. It was our third meeting. It is unrealistic to think you will have a happy family. You shouldn't place such expectations on the little boy.

I was confused. I'm sure my eyebrows were knitted in a WTF frown. I glanced at Daniel. Was I hearing things right? They didn't want us to hope to have a happy family? Were they hoping we were dreaming of providing the little boy with a shitty life? An unhappy family experience? If that was the case wouldn't they have just left him with his biological family? It's not as if we were expecting a family with no issues. That's not what "happy family" means.

We tried to clarify. We explained that we knew there would be many issues - more than we could possibly understand – but that we hoped to provide the little boy with a relatively happy life despite any issues we would face.

Regardless of the warning of unrealistic expectations, which now seemed so long ago, Daniel and I still dreamed of a happy family. We were not being unrealistic. We often discussed the not-so-happy issues we knew would be part of our family, but we believed in having happy times too. Neither Daniel nor I would believe that the little boy was incapable of happy times. We had witnessed many happy moments when he was in kindergarten.

"I'm building an anchor," he had told me in his real voice. There was just myself and one other child there. The boys and girls had been at their grade one orientation day. It was the first Friday in June. The little boy was one of two children still waiting to be picked up. My heart broke for him.

He was playing at the back of the grade one classroom. He was connecting brightly colored pieces of plastic chain together. They wrapped around the leg of a nearby desk and jutted out into the aisle. "for my boat," he continued.

"Wow," I admired. "Must be a pretty big boat." "It's a ship," he told me. The other little boy who had been playing beside him added a "me too," as I admired his work as well. "My Grampy built a boat," the little boy told me. Grampy was the little boy's foster father. They were exceptionally close. The little boy thought of his foster parents as grandparents.

"Did you help?" I asked. No response. The boy immediately turned his eyes back to his chain and continued to work. I wondered if I had said something wrong. Before I could decide if

that was in fact the case, I felt someone standing behind me. I turned to see the grade one teacher behind me. She smiled as me as if she appreciated my attempt to communicate with the little boy - the little "mute" boy. I smiled as I stood up. I shot the little boy a quick wink before leaving the room.

He and I would be the only two who were aware of our conversation about the boat. The other little child had been there. He had heard us talking. But he didn't have the same awareness of exactly what had transpired or how meaningful it had been for the little boy to have talked to me.

I left the room. I went across the hall to Daniel's classroom. He was talking with his mother who had come to pick up his niece from orientation. She had had a great day. She was smiling from ear to ear and filling her grandmother in on the day's events.

Daniel followed her into the orientation classroom as she continued her recital of the day's events. The little boy was still there but his playmate had been picked up. The little boy was playing by himself in the classroom as the orientation teacher was saying good-bye to the other little boy.

"How would you guys like to come and see my fish?" Daniel asked his niece and the little

boy. The little boy looked up. He nodded his head and left his anchor. He followed Daniel and his niece back to Daniel's room. Daniel's niece perched herself on Daniel's knee as he squatted down to point out the various fish in his aquarium. The little boy stood beside them. I squatted down on the other side of the tank. I could see the little fish schooling behind the castle inside the tank. "Can you see them?" I asked the little boy. He shook his head. "Come look over here," I suggested. The little boy came over to me. I pointed to the back of the tank and he bent down in front of me to look where I was pointing. "Ooooh," he admired.

I was shocked to hear him speak in more than a whisper given the audience. Daniel and I were there, along with Daniel's niece and his mother. Daniel and I exchanged a look and a smile. Daniel reached out and gave my hand a quick squeeze.

We decided to call the adoption top lady again. We deliberated about calling her two days in a row but she had not returned our call the day before. We decided we'd call after school, that would give her all day to return our call before we tried her again. At the end of the school day Daniel came up to my office. We first called our messaging center. We didn't want to call her if she had already tried returning our call.

"You have no new messages."

I shot Daniel a quick roll of my eyes and dialed the adoption top lady's number. An unfamiliar voice answered. I asked for the adoption top lady. She was busy. Did I want to leave a message? I left my name and number again. "Will she know what this is pertaining to?" "Yes," I almost laughed. Of course she'd know what this was pertaining to.

The rest of the day passed. We did not hear from the adoption top lady.

The next day we decided to send her an e-mail. We went online to see if we could find an email address for her. Sure enough we found one under the government adoption website. We put together a quick, pleasant e-mail inquiring about the status of our situation.

Within an hour of sending the e-mail we received a phone call. It was the adoption top lady. She was "returning our call" but had not received our e-mail. I was somewhat skeptical about this given the timing of the phone call, but that was neither here nor there.

We inquired about where things stood. She had finally received and reviewed the final report - edited and revised. The whole edited-and-revised issue still bothered me. I still wonder exactly how many revisions had been made to account for the letters sent in by our family and friends. To discredit their claims as well as the ones Daniel and I had made in our letter as well. Not that it mattered. It was too late to go back in time and hear the original report. We would just have to deal with whatever this new and improved report would hold for us.

The adoption top lady was planning on scheduling a meeting to go over the report and review the decision that had been made. I wondered if Daniel and I would be present. If we would be able to present our case to whoever would be in attendance. She continued before I could even voice the possibility. Present at the meeting would be the two workers, the head lady, herself and a fifth person we had not heard of before. Great. No fans in that club.

The mystery lady was like a systems manager. She would be needed if our case was to be re-opened and new workers were to be reassigned. Well that at least made it sound as if that were still a possibility.

We requested to have the letters we had put in our file reviewed at the meeting as well. At least that way our views and interests would be recognized. Her response was neutral. I didn't know if that meant that our letters would be presented or not. Either way her response was such that it left little room for questions.

At this point we hated getting our hopes up. After everything we had been through it would almost be easier not to. But despite our best attempt, even the smallest possibilities gave us great hope.

CHAPTER 9

THE MEETING

THE HEAD LADY WOULD GET back to us regarding the date of the meeting - not that we would be invited - but just to let us know. She was hoping to schedule it before July 1st, as the systems manager would be on holidays after that and there was no telling how long it would take to get everyone together between summer holidays and hectic schedules.

It was safer to assume the meeting would not happen before the first of July. The way things had been going so far in the process, waiting seemed to be the one thing we could be sure of.

Thankfully the end of school kept Daniel and I relatively pre-occupied. Between reports, report cards, end of year activities, and managerial stuff, Daniel and I had little free time. Little free time meant little time for dwelling. Little time for dwelling was good.

After celebrating the last day of school with the students we had a bit more free time on our hands. Once again we found ourselves dreaming about the possibilities of what might be. Of the family we might become in the near future - near future being a relative term of course.

It had been a few weeks since we had last spoken to the adoption top lady and she had not called to inform us of the meeting. As had become the routine, we decided to call her to inquire. The phone call was surprisingly upbeat and the timeline was equally as surprising. The meeting would take place before the systems manager's holidays. It would take place on Wednesday - the last day of school for teachers. She would call us back after the meeting.

I envisioned a conference room with a large table and a dozen or so chairs squeezed in all around. I was actually envisioning the same room that Daniel and I had first met the adoption top lady in. It had been a sterile room with little visual stimulation. I imagined piles of papers strewn across the table and heated debates as to what the perfect match for the little boy would look like. I pictured people bickering back and forth over the little things. The many little things which led to the decision that Daniel and I were not a match for the little boy.

I wondered if it would be like a jury deciding a court trial. Would the decision have to be unanimous? Would people argue their points back and forth until exhaustion? Would anyone concede? I wondered how long the meeting would last and who would advocate for who. It was sad really - but I was assuming someone would advocate for Daniel and me.

Daniel didn't have as vivid an idea about his expectations. He didn't see stacks of papers or heated debates. He wasn't really sure what it would look like. But more specifically, he didn't know what it would result in.

Daniel and I often discussed the "what ifs" for each possible outcome. The "what if" they say no. And the "what if" they say yes. Either was almost too much to fathom. The yes would not mean that Daniel and I would definitively be parents to the little boy. The yes would mean that Daniel and I would need to undergo more assessment to determine whether or not we would be appropriate parents for the little boy. The yes would allow us to dream a little longer. The no would be devastating.

Daniel and I had lived through one no already. It would crush us to have to live through another. Especially if it meant the end of the road. We were unsure of where we could turn next, or if there was even anywhere else to consider. We had discussed the possibilities of pleading our case to the Minister of Health. We didn't know where that would get us. We had also wondered if legal counsel would be beneficial. We had always decided we would cross those bridges at a later time if needed.

I wondered why it was so hard. There were so many children in need of good homes - so many children in need of kind, loving parents. I wondered how many other people had gone through the process and ended up like Daniel and me. I wondered if they fought the decision or accepted their fate. I wondered how their stories ended.

Daniel and I did not want to accept a fate that was unfair and unfounded.

Although there weren't many of them, the days passed slowly.

For the past few years Daniel and I always hosted an evening event on June 30th. Our parents and our siblings, as well as their children, were invited to our house for an evening of food, fireworks, and fun. My brother is not usually in attendance. He is not one for large family gatherings and often times his work schedule does not allow for his participation. My sisters and their families are usually present, and Daniel's family as well as my parents, are always a definite.

The last day of school for teachers always ended at noon and Daniel and I wanted to pick up a few last minute things for the evening. The menu was always finger foods, with the exception of a crock of homemade baked beans that was always supplied by my father. We also wanted to make sure there were some gluten-free options for my mother. She had recently been diagnosed with celiac disease and was unable to eat anything with any form or amount of gluten in it. Despite her dietary condition, a feast was always had by all.

We wondered if it was a sign that we would learn our fate on what we had always considered to be "family day". We wondered if the fireworks would be celebrating more than just the beginning of summer. Daniel and I talked quickly and excitedly about the possibilities of all we may have to celebrate as we rushed up and down the grocery store aisles.

We dreamed about the possibility of the little boy being part of family day in years to come. We imagined pointing up at the sky with the explosion of each blast of color. We pictured him playing with our nieces and nephews and eating marshmallows off a stick over the fire pit. We tossed a big bag of large, brightly colored marshmallows into the cart and headed for the checkout.

We were nervous as we left the grocery store. We almost raced to the vehicle. We had been watching the clock all morning and could hardly wait to get home and find out the news. We didn't know if she would have already called, or if she would have left a message. We had initially assumed that she would have called us on our cell phone if she had phoned. However, we had the cell phone on all morning and had not received any calls.

We weren't sure if we were supposed to call her or if she was supposed to call us. At this point it didn't matter much. We had decided that if we didn't hear from her at some point in the morning, we would call her when we got home. Our nervousness was probably readable on the speedometer. I'm usually the faster driver of the two of us, but today Daniel was driving with a led foot. I suppose it could have gone either way. Slow driving could also be considered nervousness. Perhaps anxiousness or hopefulness were better words.

I didn't realize I had been holding my breath until Daniel turned the vehicle into our driveway. As the engine stilled I could feel my heart pounding. I let out a long, slow breath. This was it. Daniel grinned at me.

He understood. He always understood. He reached out and took my hand. We each took a deep breath. We exhaled together. Relax. Breathe. Calm.

We wasted no time taking our groceries into the house. I quickly put everything away while Daniel took the dog out for his afternoon pee. We were nervous. We were stalling. I flitted around straightening things until Daniel came in. The dog ran over to greet me. I bend down and kissed his head. "I know," I responded to him. "Today's the big day."

CHAPTER 10

ANOTHER VERDICT

WHEN THERE WAS NOTHING LEFT to busy ourselves with we stopped. We stood in the middle of the room looking for something, anything - pillows to straighten, cat hair to pick off the chair, anything. There was nothing left. The house was spotless, we were ready for family, and it was time to phone. Exhale.

Daniel and I both understood the gravity of this phone call. This was it. There was no going backwards. This phone call would make or break everything we had been dreaming of. Deep breath.

Daniel dialed the number. His hands were shaking. I wiped my hands down the sides of my shorts and looked up at him as the phone began to ring. "Hello." It was her. No receptionist, no answering machine, no waiting. My breath caught in my throat. This was it.

Neither Daniel nor I had been ready for her response. Despite all our conversations, dreams, and discussions; reality has a way of diverting all plans and preparations.

I sat down. Daniel put the phone back. We looked at each other. I don't know which of us exhaled first.

I jumped up and avoided his eyes. People would soon be arriving for family night. No time to talk or plan. Just time to avoid. To make busy. To climb inside myself and cry.

My chest hurt. That's probably where the whole "broken heart" phrase comes from. I wondered if you could die from a broken heart. I didn't suppose so. But I could see why people would want to.

There was nothing I wanted more than to grab Daniel and hold him tight. I knew he was as devastated as I was. But I couldn't. I knew once we opened those flood gates we would be done for the day. Neither of us could afford to be done for the day with our families already on their way. We would avoid our broken hearts for the remainder of the day.

"It's not because of you, it's because of the little boy's needs," she had told Daniel on the phone. How cliché was that? I felt like I was being dumped in some junior high episode of "it's not you it's me." "But you should meet with the man and his supervisor to go over the final report," she continued. She thought that would be helpful. I didn't see the point. Their no was final. What good would reading the report do? And I didn't know if I could bring myself to sit in front of the man and once again go over all the

reasons why Daniel and I were not chosen as a match for the little boy.

"It's confidential," she had answered when Daniel had tried to inquire about the issue. Of course it was. That's pretty convenient. No need to come up with any answers or justifications. It's confidential.

We would call the man's supervisor next week. That would give us time to talk. Time to think. And time to breathe. But for the time being, we had a party to live through.

We decided not to make the big announcement that evening. As supportive as our families would be, we were not ready to have our heartache be the topic of conversation - no matter how well-meaning everyone was. Plus, we didn't want to put a damper on the evening. Everyone always had such a great time, and for the first time ever my brother was going to be coming. That made me happy and sad all at the same time.

I knew the evening would be tough. We would be surrounded by children. Not that that was a bad thing. We loved children. And our nieces and nephews were among the children we loved most in the world. But tonight it would be hard. It would be hard to hold them and hug them and love them without thinking about the child we would not be able to hold and hug and love. Tonight every hug and every tug of the hand would tear at our hearts.

Daniel's youngest niece would be especially hard to see tonight. She had staked a claim to me from the first time I met her. I belonged to her. As far as she was concerned I was hers and hers alone. Hers to climb on, hers to cling to, hers to lead around by the hand, and hers to share fond moments with. Often times she would just pull me into the living room and curl up on my lap to watch tv. Other times she would lead me around the house showing me things she thought I might not have seen before. There were times she would drag me outside to play audience to the new tricks she learned on the trampoline or on her bike, and there were times she would just hunker down beside me and nestle close. Regardless of the activity, I was hers.

My nieces and nephews were fond of Daniel and me as well, just not to the point of ownership. They would run straight at us and jump into our arms at the last minute, or repeatedly place small rubber insects in our hair and wait for us to dance around waving our arms and screaming in a fit of fear which delighted them every time. Often times they would show us new dance moves or things they had seen on tv, or show us pictures and crafts they had created especially for us.

Our younger nieces and nephews were not old enough to appreciate relationships of this nature, but even watching them take unsteady steps toward us would be enough to tug at our heart strings tonight.

This would be the first time that my brother's son will have been to our house. We interacted with him often at his house or at my parent's house, but I was curious to see how he would interact with the larger extended crowd.

Daniel went to pick up some Kentucky Fried Chicken before our guests started arriving. I was sure he would appreciate the alone time. Daniel usually processed things by asking what we joke about as being a million questions. But there was no one to ask the questions to anymore. It was a done deal. We would not be adopting the little boy and all the questions in the world would not change that. I knew that Daniel would use this time to sort through his thoughts and to try to harness his emotions.

I knew Daniel as well as he knew me. I knew he would drive slowly by the church graveyard on his way to Kentucky. He would bless himself as he always did. But tonight he would look past the church and into the graveyard where we had buried his grandmother less than a year earlier. He would talk to her, confide in her and ask for her strength to get him through the evening. He would then whisper happy birthday to her and tell her how much he missed her.

She had been a huge part of Daniel's life. She had lived with Daniel's family his whole life. She had left an unfillable void in the family when she had passed away. Today's news would re-open that void for Daniel. There would be a fresh wound in his heart where a loved one should be. Tonight would be especially hard for him.

I did my best to scurry around while he was gone. I wiped down the countertops and table for what felt like the thousandth time. I arranged and re-arranged the food and the snacks. I folded the napkins and placed them in neat piles. I sorted the cutlery and re-rinsed the glasses.

Tires. Exhale. I was out the door before I even stopped to see who had arrived. It didn't matter. I was just thrilled to have someone to occupy my mind. I smiled as my oldest niece, only five years old, jumped out of the van and ran toward me with open arms. I darted down the front steps and met her halfway, sweeping her up into a hug and spinning her around. "Hi Aunt Morgan," she said in her beautiful sing song way. "Hi honey," I responded as my heart felt its first crack.

I set her back down and we went back to the van to help my sister with her other two girls. Her second oldest, only two, was calling out hellos from her car seat and her youngest, only seven months, sat contently in her car seat as her mother unfastened the straps.

It didn't take long for people to start arriving. Daniel's family arrived only minutes after my sister, and the house was already filled with the sound of hustle and bustle and children playing. Daniel returned next and was followed in by my parents and my aunt. My aunt and I had a very special relationship. Her love was unconditional and undeniable. She was well-intentioned but was always working towards bettering herself as a person. She was a wonderful person - I did not understand her quest for betterment.

My younger sister and her family arrived shortly thereafter. She had three children. Her oldest boy was not school age yet and she had a set of twins even younger.

Her oldest son loved the excitement of a big crowd, and spent time interacting with everyone. He was a cutie pie through and through - and a little charmer to boot. The twins were a little shyer and spent their time between their parents and grandparents.

The evening was pretty informal. People were mingling and snacking. Some were discussing politics and others were talking about latest movies. The kitchen and living room were full and there were others lingering on the patio and in the yard.

Daniel's oldest niece, thirteen, was kicking around a soccer ball and had asked me to join her. She was a great girl. She was smart, pretty, athletic, and had a great sense of humor. She and I often kidded and joked around, but other times we had some pretty serious conversations about boys, peer pressure, and past scars. She kept me entertained for much of the evening, kicking the soccer ball around and later helping me relocate Dad's fireworks away from the birdhouses in the back yard.

My brother and his son arrived a little later. They both came out to the back yard while waving a hello to everyone; my nephew's wave accompanied by shrill hellos to "grampy" and me. "Hey stranger," I said to my brother as I gave him a big hug. "Hey sis," he said hugging me back. I didn't know if he squeezed me exceptionally hard, or if my heart was already weakened by the cracks of the evening, but I wanted to cry right there on the spot.

My brother and I had always been close. When he was born I took ownership of him. He was MY brother and I was HIS sister. Despite an age difference of seven years, we remained close all during our childhood and into adulthood.

I was close with all my siblings, and I had a unique relationship with each of them. My oldest sister and I were very similar and as such we got along very well. Even when we didn't see eye to eye, we managed to agree to disagree - neither subsiding their views in the slightest. My younger sister was a very kind and compassionate person. Despite being younger then me she would often look out for my feelings and stick up for me if she thought someone was pressuring me. She was aware of my guilt complex and always did her best to remain cognizant of it.

I was close with my parents as well. My mother was a very thoughtful and genuine person. She was always doing thoughtful things for people. My father was a very practical man. He was a jack of all trades and did not take things sitting down. I enjoyed his determination. I had grown up to be a compliment of my mother and my father.

Daniel's parents were very similar. His father was a very handy man like mine, and was able to turn his hand to any project. His mother was the emotional balance of the family and was always there for people when they needed her. She was a very kind and compassionate soul.

Daniel was the perfect blend of his parents. He was an exceptionally loyal man with the heart of a lion. Daniel went above and beyond to support the people he was closest to. He stood up for what he believed in and inspired the people around him to do the same. Daniel is a wonderful man. I love Daniel.

Daniel's sister was very similar to Daniel in many ways. Much like Daniel, she was not afraid to speak her mind or to stand up for what she believed in. She kept her softer side more hidden than Daniel did, but it was there nonetheless.

Daniel's sister was also a very talented musician. She had gotten that from their father. Before the fireworks she played the guitar while some of us sang. The musical venue consisted of the golden oldies. Those who didn't sing kept beat in some fashion or another.

All of Daniel's nieces were musically inclined. They all played multiple instruments and took part in lessons and concerts. Daniel's middle niece was more the performer than the other two. She often accompanied her mother at ceilidhs and concerts. She was a sweet girl - only nine years old. She was as kind as she was compassionate but also had the wit and spunk of her mother.

I was enjoying the distractions. It was nice to get caught up in a moment and not think about the devastating news we had received just hours earlier. Daniel seemed to be lost in the evening as well. I was glad. I knew what was coming for us and I was glad we were able to get some enjoyment out of the evening.

As the sun disappeared we gathered around the patio doors to enjoy the fireworks. I borrowed a second lighter to help my father light off the various packages of fireworks he had purchased on his last trip South.

My brother ended up rescuing me from the embarrassment of not being able to effectively manipulate the safety apparatus on the lighter. We switched spots. He became my father's second in command and I watched his son.

It was nice to wrap my arms around a little boy and ooh and aah at the lights and sounds of each explosion. He squealed in delight as the sky lit up, and screamed "Again Grampy! Again Daddy!" each time the color began to fade from the sky. He would have loved for the fireworks to last all night.

I would have loved for them to last all night as well. But eventually the last of the colored sparks disappeared from the sky and people began packing up and getting ready to leave. Daniel and I found one another and thanked our guests for a wonderful evening.

As the last of the visitors disappeared down the driveway, Daniel slowly closed the door and reached for my hand. I took his hand and rested my head on his shoulder. No more avoiding. Daniel kissed my forehead as tears began making their way down the sides of my face.

CHAPTER 11

THE DAY AFTER

DANIEL AND I JUST PICKED at our breakfast. Neither of us was hungry and neither of us knew what to say. It didn't seem like there was anything we could say. We would not be adopting the little boy. As nicely as anyone could have said it, it still hurt. It still hurt and it still seemed like the wrong decision.

I looked up from my cup of coffee. Daniel was watching me. I could see the pain in his eyes. "Sucks huh?" I asked trying to be matter-of-fact. "Yup. It sucks." Daniel agreed.

The flood gates opened and Daniel and I talked for hours. We talked about the decision. We shared our disappointment, our frustrations, and our heartbreak. We relived the dreams of being parents to the little boy. We smiled over all the things the little boy might have done or might have enjoyed had he been with us the evening before.

As much as our dream was over, neither of us wanted to let it die. We wanted to continue to fight for the little boy. We wanted to prove our abilities to the people in charge of the decision and force them to understand that they had made a mistake.

Daniel and I both knew that was an unrealistic expectation. The department didn't make mistakes. And even when they did - they didn't. We knew it was unrealistic to believe that anyone in the department would admit to a mistake having been made. We were right back to the CYA philosophy. This mistake would be supported by everyone in the system, that's how CYA works. There really was no where left to turn.

We decided that our next step, the only step we had left, was to schedule a meeting with the man and his supervisor. We would follow the top lady's recommendation of reading the report. Maybe there was something in the report that would help clarify things for us. Maybe there really was some confidential need on the part of the little boy that Daniel and I could not facilitate.

Neither Daniel nor I would push to adopt the little boy if it was not in his best interest. We loved him - as strange as that may sound - and just wanted the best for him. If there was another family out there to give him everything he needed then we would be the first to wish him all the best.

But the fact of the matter still remained that there was no family out there for him. A match had not yet been found. The little boy was still living in the limbo of foster care. Still waiting to be place in his "forever home".

"You would rather him bounce around in foster care until he's eighteen then to have a life with

us?" Daniel had said the words. That hadn't even occurred to me. I was still struggling to accept what they had said. "That's right," she had challenged back. "And the time we could have used to find him a match, we spent assessing you." I was shocked. I couldn't believe she had the gall to say something so horrendous to us. The man didn't say anything. He didn't step in to soften her blow. Nothing. He just watched us as she continued to take notes. Daniel was angry. His original acceptance of the decision was crumbling. He had been able to accept the decision because he had believed a better home had been found for the little boy. This was not the case. It was becoming increasingly more difficult for Daniel to understand and accept what was being said. The decision was horrible. This meeting was horrible. The fact that the woman was taking notes was horrible. I have never wanted to leave a room so quickly in all my life.

We phoned the supervisor and got her voice mail. We decided to call back the following day instead of leaving a message. We had not experienced a lot of success with messages so far and decided it would be easier for us just to call back.

We called the supervisor again the next day. It was Friday. She was still not in. Perhaps she was on holidays.

We decided to wait until Monday to call her back. If she still wasn't in we would leave a message.

Things remained relatively busy at home. Daniel had to meet with his thesis advisor in the next few days. Because of a hectic schedule of his own, his advisor was only available some 2000 km away. It would be a twenty hour drive for us, but we were excited at the thought of a summer trip. Planning for the trip became another distraction for us. We were able to revert to "trip mode" when things got too painful.

It was hard to deal with a pain you didn't understand. It was even harder to deal with pain when such a large part of yourself was still hoping for a miracle. Our miracle would have to be put on hold until after our trip.

At the beginning of the week we tried once again to get a hold of the supervisor. Again we got a hold of her voice mail. This time we left a message. We explained who we were and requested a call back. We maintained an upbeat and cheery disposition, despite the anxiety and heartbreak we were feeling. We left our cell phone number even though we were not sure when she would return our call. But if she did, we didn't want to miss it if we were gone on our trip when she phoned us back.

The trip was fun. It was nice to get away. Despite leaving home, we took a lot of our hopes and dreams with us. We often talked about what the trip would look like if the little boy was with us. We wondered if he'd love traveling, where we would stop, and the places we would take him. We talked about him when we were walking hand in hand through the malls. We talked about him when we were visiting new places and eating at exciting restaurants.

He was especially present in our conversations when we visited the Rain Forest Café restaurant. We knew from kindergarten that he loved dinosaurs.

"I'm not afraid of dinosaurs," he had said flipping through the pages of a dinosaur encyclopedia. "Not even that one?" I had gasped pointing to the scariest dinosaur on the page. "Nope," he had answered bravely, "not even that one," he said turning the page to reveal a large, scary looking dinosaur with sharp jagged teeth and large talon like claws. He looked up at me like a tiny knight who had just killed the ferocious beast. I smiled down at him. "Hmmmmm," I mused, "what about…this one?" I said turning the pages quickly to reveal a giant and vicious looking horned beast. "Nope," he said in the most serious and solemn voice, "not even that one."

Daniel and I looked around the restaurant in awe. There were large, life-like creatures everywhere. Gorillas beat their chests in the vines of the jungle décor, snakes and other creatures protruded from trees and other realistic looking vegetation, and smoke curled and bubbled from other areas of the restaurant. Massive fish tanks lined the entrance to the eating area and extended overhead to create an aquarium archway. The entire experience was fantastical and we daydreamed about the little boy's reaction to such an amazing creation.

It was fun to day dream with Daniel. He understood exactly what I was thinking and feeling as I did with him. We were able to build on one another's imagination and create a wonderful dream that we hoped to one day fulfill. We talked about all the things we would love to do with the little boy and all the places we would like to one day take him.

We talked about someday taking him to Disney World. Daniel and I had been there twice, both times as adults. Disney was an amazing experience and we could only imagine the magic that Disney would hold for a child. We talked about what park the little boy might like the most and guessed as to which attractions would be his favorites.

No matter where we went or what we did, the little boy was always on the surface of our experiences. Even in our down time we talked about the little boy. We wondered what tv shows he would find entertaining, or whether or not he would slide down the three story waterslide at the hotel.

At the end of the day Daniel and I would always retire together. He would watch sports and I would curl up at his side and fall asleep with my head on his chest. Daniel and I knew that we would have a long and happy life together. We just hoped we would be able to share that life with the little boy.

There were only a few days left before we would return home. We still had not heard back from the supervisor. We decided to e-mail the top lady to ask for the supervisor's e-mail address. We heard back from the top lady immediately, and promptly sent an e-mail to the supervisor. We were anxious to make an appointment to meet. We were anxious to keep the process going as a means of keeping our dream alive.

We did not receive a reply to our e-mail. We waited two days and left another phone message. We were again pleasant and cheery on the phone. We did not want to alienate the supervisor by being frustrated with the difficulty in getting a hold of her.

8:00 am the next morning she returned our call. She sounded very kind and compassionate on the phone. She was friendly and apologetic. She felt badly about not getting a hold of us earlier. We arranged to meet at 1:00 pm the following week. This would give Daniel and me a chance to get home and get settled, and it would give her a chance to arrange things with the man.

Within minutes she phoned us back and asked to change the time to 11:00 am. She wanted to ensure that we had ample time to go over things. The man had a meeting later that afternoon and she didn't want that to cause our meeting to be cut short. She seemed like such a nice lady. I hoped our meeting would be productive.

Daniel and I had a wonderful trip home. We enjoyed the travel. We talked openly about our lives and about what our lives would look like with and without children.

Although Daniel and I both wanted to share our lives with children, we understood that there was a strong possibility that this may not happen.

We didn't want to become another statistic - a couple who breaks up because they could not handle the stress of the disappointment of broken dreams. We talked about ways we would work through our disappointments and hurts if in fact our dreams were not meant to be.

Time heals all wounds. We knew that. And we also knew that we would be there for each other during that passing of time, no matter how hard it turned out to be. I loved Daniel and he loved me. Ours would be a story of love conquers all.

CHAPTER 12

ANOTHER MEETING

TIME SEEMED TO PASS QUICKLY between the time we left the hotel and our meeting with the supervisor and the man. It was a little surreal to be sitting in that waiting room once again. The last time Daniel and I had been here had not been so wonderful.

We had sat in the waiting room well past our appointment time wondering with all our might about the decision to come. We had held one another's hands and anticipated that dreadful decision. Daniel had been sure we would be accepted as a match for the little boy. I was more skeptical. I had not gotten the greatest vibe from the woman and the man was rather nonchalant. Daniel was more focused on what we had to offer the little boy than he was with their reactions to us. He knew that the workers needed to be clinical. He also knew that I would find the clinical approach to be rather cold and disengaging. Despite either of our thoughts on the situation, neither of us had been prepared to deal with the pain we endured that day.

I was unsure about how I felt. I had felt a tightening in the pit of my stomach as we entered the waiting room that day. We sat in the same seats as we had months earlier. We held hands, just as we did the last time we waited in that office.

The receptionist was not the same. This receptionist was friendly. She had shoulder length curly hair and she was slightly plump. She smiled at us and chatted about the beautiful weather. She was a welcome change from our last experience. Her personality and presence made the office feel somewhat more welcoming.

I wondered if we would be kept waiting. Daniel gave my hand a quick squeeze. I was sure he was reading my mind. We took quick and curious glances at the people who stepped in and out of the receptionist's office. We wondered which of those people, if any, was the supervisor.

Although she had a young, sweet voice, I was expecting an older lady. The supervisor had been a social worker for my grandmother many, many moons ago when my grandparent's were foster parents. It had been years since my grandparents had passed away and decades before that that they were foster parents. The time frame alone allowed me to assume the supervisor would be a little old lady with white hair and wrinkles of experience.

I was surprised when an average sized lady, who appeared to be in her late forties or early fifties, came to the door and introduced herself as the supervisor. She had warm dark eyes that matched her dark brown hair. She was wearing a necklace with a large pendant that looked to be made out of some sort of sea shell.

She guided us to an office down the hall and to the left. It was the same office in which Daniel and I had first met the man and the woman. The man met us in the hallway and followed us to the office. He extended a friendly hello and commented on Daniel's hair having grown since the last time he'd seen us.

Daniel and I sat by the window in the same seats we had sat in so many months earlier. The supervisor sat by the door and the man sat in front of the desk, the same place he had sat so many months earlier.

The supervisor spoke first. She welcomed us and said she was pleased to meet us. She seemed nervous. Her hands went from her necklace to the ring on her finger and then circled around each other as if she were massaging her fingers.

Although she was kind and soft spoken, she seemed to talk a bit in circles. She repeated several times about the emotions of couples in our situation and the tenderness taken when dealing with such situations. I was a little surprised by her nervousness. The man didn't jump in. He looked back and forth from the lady to Daniel and me.

The lady finally asked what Daniel and I would like to talk about. I was a little surprised by the question.

I was under the understanding that Daniel and I were there to read the report. Her question didn't reflect this understanding.

"The top lady suggested that reading the report would be a good starting place," I began. I didn't get to finish my thought. The lady began explaining to us again about emotions and things like that. She talked about dealing with reports and reacting to the things we would read. She talked in circles again as she repeated her cautions over and over. Her hands didn't stop moving the entire time she spoke.

I felt badly. I knew the report was going to be rough. Despite the report, I felt badly for the supervisor. She seemed like a genuinely nice woman and she was so obviously uncomfortable. Perhaps nervous was a better word. She was expecting that Daniel and I were not going to react favorably to the report.

I glanced at Daniel. I couldn't tell if he was aware of the lady's nervousness. The man watched me. He glanced from me to Daniel and back to me again. I avoided making eye contact with him. I was still so hurt by everything that had happened that I didn't really like him very much. Whether he had been the primary decider of our future of not, he was certainly associated with that heartbreak.

I looked back at the supervisor. I could still see the man out of the corner of my eye. He seemed unaware that the lady was repeating herself. Either that or he was okay with all the repetition. Daniel and I sat patiently and listened to her. It was a good fifteen minutes between the time we asked to read the report and the time it was actually given to us.

I was anticipating a pretty negative report. The time lapse, along with the repetition and nervousness were a relatively strong indication that the report was not going to be pretty.

I glanced over at Daniel again. He caught my eye. He was aware that the supervisor was stalling. He was also aware that this did not bode well for the report.

> *The woman had also been stalling four months earlier when Daniel and I had been there to find out the devastating reality that we would not be parents to the little boy. She had talked for about five minutes about not wanting to dilly-dally about the result. She had gone on and on about feeling it was only fair to just come out with it instead of keeping people waiting. She had not been aware that all her talk about not wanting to keep people waiting had just kept us waiting.*
>
> *I had clued in almost immediately that it was not good news. There is no need to cushion people for good news. She was cushioning the delivery of the news. Cushioning was not good. The news was not good. We would not be the little boy's parents.*

More cushioning. The supervisor was cushioning the report. Neither of us interrupted her. Nor did the man.

He sat and watched as she spoke. He watched us more than he watched her despite the fact that we were not the ones speaking. He did the same the last time. Déjà vu. The report would not be good.

CHAPTER 13

THE REPORT

I HOPED ALL THE CUSHIONING had been preparing Daniel. I couldn't tell and I didn't want to glance at him too often.

When the cushioning came to an end the man scurried out of the room to get the report. The supervisor reassured us that the report would not be kept at the office. She ensured that all copies of the report are shredded with only the original kept on file in the central office. She was pleased to tell us that she had made special arrangements to keep our report there on the knowledge that we would be coming in to look at it.

The explanation seemed to be more than we needed to know. She was still nervous and her chatter seemed to be an awkward way to fill the time until the man returned with the report. Daniel and I thanked her for her thoughtfulness.

The man returned and handed the report to the supervisor. She once again reminded us of the nature of the report and that the purpose of the meeting was to clarify any issue Daniel and I may have with the report.

She handed the report to Daniel and me to read. We moved closer together so we could read the report together. The man and the supervisor carried on a somewhat trivial conversation - vacation time, the weather, office dynamics - as Daniel and I read through the report.

There was no cushioning within the report itself. There was a brief paragraph or two explaining how Daniel and I came to be aware of the little boy and our hopes to adopt him. After that we delved immediately into Daniel - who he was, why he was, what he was.

There were no holds barred in the report. I was immediately caught off guard by the number of assumptions and interpretations included in the report. I had been a special education teacher for years and had some training in writing reports and documentations. The number one thing I had always been told was "stick to the facts." Reports and documents were no place for speculation or assumptions.

Obviously the man and the woman had not had the same training. Much of the report contained their reactions and interpretations of what had been said instead of the actual comments themselves. There were the odd set of quotation marks surrounding words and phrases that had not been our wording but their paraphrasing of things they felt were pertinent or concerning.

I pointed to several things as I read. I wanted to make sure Daniel was seeing what I was seeing. I drew his attention to things I would bring up later.

I felt badly for Daniel as I read through the section of the report that pertained to him. Many of the things that had been written were unfair statements and suggestions that were neither justified nor appropriate. One of the first things that caught my eye was the statement "Daniel doesn't speak much about his father. This will need to be looked into at a later date." I was appalled when I read that sentence.

Anyone who hadn't been at the meeting in which the man and the woman had asked Daniel about his family would read this report and suspect that there was an issue between Daniel and his father. This was completely not the case. Daniel and his father had an excellent relationship and a great respect for one another. The truth of the matter was that during our second meeting with the man and the woman - the second of three meetings - Daniel was not asked much about his father.

Our meetings had been rushed for our benefit and we had known and understood that. We did our best to answer all their questions as precisely as possible. We wanted to give them as much information as we could in the short time frame we were working with. We didn't want to get bogged down on stories or information that may not have been relevant.

We had been made very aware of time during our first meeting with the man and the woman. We had rushed down after work, arriving at their office at 4:00 pm. By five o'clock the alarm on the man's watch had gone off twice and he kept glancing at the time. We felt badly for keeping them past supper time and tried to answer their questions as quickly as possible. As we left that meeting I had apologized for keeping them late. The man expressed confusion about my apologies. I explained that I had been aware of his alarm ringing and that I hoped we hadn't made him late for another appointment.

We thought nothing more about it as we left that evening. Our next two meetings had been squeezed in between busy schedules and again time was not a commodity we had a lot of. The third meeting - the meeting to explore who, why, and what I was - was held in the morning. Daniel and I had taken the morning off work and were to be back to work by 12:00. The weather had been somewhat blustery that day and the man and woman had been delayed by drifting snow and bad roads. Our meeting - which would have been no more than 1 hour and 45 minutes - was cut short by 35 minutes. Again we felt the need to be as brief as possible so as to answer as many questions as we could in a very short amount of time.

I could not believe that Daniel was being penalized for the time crunch! "Daniel did not talk much about his father"? What a load of crap! How about "Daniel was not asked much about his father," that would have been a more accurate depiction.

As I read through the report I remembered how much I had hated the man and the woman the last time I had seen them. This report only reaffirmed those feelings.

I pointed at the comment about Daniel and his father and made eye contact with Daniel. He was annoyed as well. We both turned our attention back to the report. Neither of us said anything. Our job at the moment was to read the report. Our rebuttals would come after the report was read.

The next jaw-dropping comment involved Daniel's religious beliefs. Daniel and I had both decided, mutually, that we would not consider invitro fertilization due to the Church's stance on artificial insemination. The man and the woman also had a stance on the issue. They commented that "although admirable," Daniel's religious beliefs were "naïve." Despite our obvious differences in religious beliefs, it is completely and utterly unacceptable to judge the religious beliefs of someone else.

Again I locked eyes with Daniel. He knew I was pissed. This report was an entire crock of shit. Things were misconstrued and misinterpreted in a very negative way. The report was not fair. Worse than that, the report was final. Final and permanent.

The section of the report that focused on Daniel had infuriated me. I would have chewed it up and swallowed it had I thought it was the only copy. Either that or I would have chewed it up and spat it at the man.

I was cautious not to make eye contact with the man or the supervisor. I wanted to keep my emotions in check. If Daniel and I had any hope of clarifying this report, we had to remain calm and level headed. Thank God that was something I was good at.

My pride in that God-given ability did not last long. The report summarized my level-headed nature as being guarded, defensive, emotionally shut-down, and other such lovely descriptors. And because of these wonderful character traits the comment was written that children would find it difficult to bond with me and to form relationships with me.

In the report I was quoted to have said that I "analyze everything." What I had actually said was that I analyze situations before I make any decisions. I had also elaborated on analyzing body language in relation to a specific issue with one of the students I was working with.

This student had special needs and was unable to interpret body language. As a result he was having difficulties in class that were becoming an issue for both he and the teacher. It was believed that the child was misbehaving and that he would not follow the teacher's directions to correct unwanted behaviors. In reality many of the teachers "directions" were given in the form of body language - pointing, motioning, proximity, eye contact, etc. - and the student was simply unaware of the implications of such actions.

Somewhere in the midst of that story I had sold myself out as "analyzing everything." I knew as soon as I had said it that the woman had misinterpreted what I had said.

"How do you think this little boy is going to react when you analyze him? How do you think he will feel to have you analyzing his every move?" "That's not what I meant." I struggled to get the words out. It was going wrong - horribly wrong. That wasn't what I was saying. I hadn't even suggested that I analyze children; I had been analyzing the body language of the teacher.

"That would be a terrible thing to do to him," she continued. She was angry with me. "I wouldn't do that to him," I tried to explain. Back-tracking. It sounded like I was back-tracking.

"Morgan is amazing with children," Daniel said coming to the rescue. "She has a wonderful rapport with children. She knows what they need and gives them the space they need to feel comfortable. She doesn't analyze them and make them feel bad."

She shook her head and continued on with her questions. She didn't believe us. There was no retracting that story and there was no clarifying what she had understood from it.

I was beyond infuriated. Every detail of our encounters had been twisted and turned into something negative. There was an anecdote about my not taking off my jacket during our first meeting. How this had alerted them from the onset of my distrust in the system and my inability to form a trusting relationship - a crucial relationship - with the social workers.

Dear God I was cold!!! It was the middle of winter and my fingers were nearly numb!!!

> *"No thanks, I'm okay," I had replied when they asked us if we wanted to take our coats off. I sat in the chair against the window. The little room was sterile. Nothing on the white walls, not much on the desk. The plain vertical blinds were pulled against either side of the window to allow the winter sun to peer into the room.*
>
> *"Would you like me to turn up the heat?" the woman had offered. "No that's fine thanks," I had returned. I am usually always colder than everyone else and I didn't mind keeping my jacket on. Besides that, I had only a light sweater on underneath and everyone else seemed more appropriately dressed for a cooler work environment.*

Had I realized at the time that my jacket was an issue I would have laid it across my lap and talked through chattering teeth. I couldn't put the shock and disbelief about what I was reading into words. Had I been expected to speak at that moment I would have been speechless.

I glanced up at Daniel. His jaw was set ever so slightly. He caught my eye and raised his eyebrow up to illustrate his disapproval with the report. I took a deep breath and continued reading.

The report continued on to describe me as being unaware. Apparently I didn't recognize how others responded to me. The example to illustrate that point was my questioning of the man's watch alarm. That action - which had occurred as an apology at the end of our meeting - had somehow been determined to be inappropriate, and this somehow suggested that I was not self-aware.

I was actually quite self-aware. The fact that I was able to read the report with a straight face was proof enough that I was not only aware of myself and my actions/emotions, but also able to keep things in check.

The report continued. Not only was I an emotionless, distrusting bitch (paraphrasing of course), but I was also a control freak. The example used to demonstrate this characteristic focused on an incident in which I had attempted to clarify something that either Daniel or I had said.

We had been talking about the actual process, about how things worked and the steps involved in adopting a child. Once the overview of the process was over we talked more specifically about the little boy and about the specific needs he may encounter as he grows older.

At one point in the conversation the man had paused mid-sentence to look at the woman. She immediately returned his look and scowled. Her first language was not English and she had told us upfront that she may misinterpret what is being said and may need to seek clarification.

"Did we say something wrong?" I had asked. "Why?" she countered. "You exchanged a pretty obvious look and I wanted to make sure it wasn't something we had said," I offered.

Yup there you have it - control freak. I shot Daniel another look and continued reading. The man and woman were still engaged in their small talk, filling in the silence as Daniel and I continued through the report.

The next few lines were dedicated to excusing my controlling nature. Not re-examining the examples and realizing that perhaps there was a motive other than a controlling nature; but explaining my need to control things in my life as being related to the fact that I was infertile.

Infertility. Another concern. More investigation needed.

Well it's certainly true that I am infertile, but that was not a surprise to Daniel or me. I had known this fact for years and had come to terms with it long ago. Daniel also knew about the situation before we had ever become involved. It had only been fair to tell him incase he would rather not invest his time and energy into a life that was not to his liking.

According to the report Daniel and I needed grief counseling because we were infertile. Our alleged grief would become a potential stumbling block. Another concern. Further investigation needed.

At this point I was forcing myself to exhale slowly and quietly. I would have loved to let out a long exasperated sigh to demonstrate my annoyance and frustration with the report, but that would not have been helpful. Not that any of my attempts to be helpful had panned out thus far. The report was proof of that.

The section regarding my family was brief. The main area of interest stemmed from my description of my father. I had described him as "not being a yes man" and as a "boat rocker" - someone who stood up for what he believed in. These quotes were both accurate. I did describe my father in that manner and also stated that I felt these qualities were admirable and worthy of being passed along to future generations.

Apparently believing these qualities to be admirable was not the response the man and woman had hoped for. Their report took on a more negative connotation and suggested that I did not admire my father but instead emulated him.

As disturbing as this was, it at least explained why they would feel I was not self-aware. It would be pretty hard to be self-aware if I was not in fact myself but some emulated version of someone else. I didn't know whether to laugh or cry. I struggled to maintain that professionals - professionally trained people - could misread so much information. Another quick glance at Daniel.

Daniel was ahead of me. He waited patiently for me to finish the page before continuing on to the next page. I finished my not-so-flattering biography.

The next page offered the smallest of reprieves. The sections on Daniel and me as individuals were complete. I took a breath and tried to mentally calm myself. I was frustrated and annoyed. Daniel and I had been grossly misunderstood and misrepresented. Another deep breath. Daniel and I continued reading.

The next section of the report dealt with Daniel and I as a couple. The report described our relationship and quoted the words "best friends." I thought that was pretty ironic being as it was the woman who had supplied that term after we described how our relationship had evolved.

I would have liked at that point to tell the man and his supervisor that it is misrepresentative to attribute a quote to someone who did not say it. I bit my tongue. Anything I said at this point would most likely be interpreted as controlling. Grrrrr.

So Daniel and I were "best friends" and we spent most of our time together. Although this began to look like a glimmer of hope - a bright spot in the report - it was quickly followed by the fact that our "interdependence" was a concern.

One portion of the report was committed to describing a questionable balance in the relationship between Daniel and me. It was written that I often "shut-down" and that Daniel was left to ask questions and voice concerns.

This was actually not the case. Daniel processes things by asking questions and presenting scenarios to better understand information as it is presented. I take everything in and process the information as a whole. I don't feel a need to ask questions until I have heard everything.

This is one of the ways that Daniel and I actually balance either other out. But they didn't ask us about that. That didn't explore why we were doing the things we were doing. They just jumped on the assumption that I was avoiding the topic and forcing Daniel to do all the talking.

I was as discouraged as I was frustrated. At that point I was about ready to leave. To just pack up my stuff and walk out. I would have loved to flick the report onto a side table - completely dismissing and disregarding it - and just walk out. The little boy. I needed to see this through for the little boy. Despite all the harsh words and the misconstrued crap in that report, I knew Daniel and I had lots of love to offer the little boy.

I looked up at Daniel again. He had already finished reading that section but was waiting to catch my eye. He looked down at me and pursed his lips ever so slightly. He then shook his head gently and rolled his eyes. We locked eyes again - reassuring one another, and then returned to the report.

The final section of the report dealt with how Daniel and I reacted to the news that we were not selected as parents for the little boy. I was quoted to have "shut down" and "glared" at the man and the woman while Daniel had shown genuine concern for the little boy. Daniel had asked about the well being of the boy and had offered that he was just happy that the little boy had found a home. That was before Daniel had realized that they had not actually found the little boy a home.

Before he had asked if they would prefer the little boy to bounce from foster home to foster home instead of living with us.

My cool responses were also noted. It was also documented that I did not display my emotions during the meeting. That part was true. I did not display my emotions. I did not cry in front of them nor did I put my broken heart on exhibit. I sat quietly, apparently glaring at them, and listening to the exchanges between Daniel, the man, and the woman.

The environment had not welcomed discussion. She had stated three times, very early on in the meeting, that she was 100% confident in her decision. Her rigid posture, along with the setting of her jaw, had made it clear that there was no room for discussion. She had made her decision and that was that. No point in arguing.

I commented only when I was asked specific questions. Her questions were cold. The repeated use of my name was patronizing. She was poking a hornets' nest. I was cool and to the point when I responded. She took out a note pad and jotted something down. I hated her with every fiber of my being.

The man didn't interject. He didn't comment on the 100% remark, nor did he clarify where he stood in his confidence in the decision.

The report wrapped up in the next few paragraphs. More assumptions into what could have been intended, insinuated, or interpreted. The facts in this report were few and far between. That was something I could comment on without defending every assumption or rationalizing areas of concern.

CHAPTER 14

THE AFTER CHAT

DANIEL AND I CLOSED THE report and handed it back to the supervisor. Their conversation ended abruptly and they turned to face us. The supervisor was smiling nervously. Her hands found one another as she asked "any questions?"

"Not yet," I replied. I knew immediately what this would suggest to them. I was going into an emotional shut down mode and forcing Daniel to handle the conversation. They were wrong. They had been wrong about that in the report and they were wrong about that now. I preferred Daniel to air any of his issues or ask any questions he had before I spoke. I would want to comment on everything, including things they may tell Daniel in their own defense.

"I have a few questions," Daniel began. I was surprised by how adamant he sounded. Not that Daniel shied away from speaking his mind. He didn't. He was just usually much better at playing the game than I was. Daniel and

I both knew that if we hoped to ever adopt a child, we would need to ensure that we did not alienate ourselves from the people who could make that happen.

I would have expected Daniel to be pleasant and to sound innocently inquisitive. I was surprised to hear the frustration in his voice, not that I didn't understand exactly where the frustration was coming from. Daniel and I had been torn apart in that report and many of the things we read were not justified. In my mind he was doing well not to sound completely irate.

Daniel didn't wait for the invite to voice his concerns. He jumped immediately to the report and began to question the list of reasons as to why Daniel and I were not suitable parents for the little boy. The list had not changed since the first time we had heard it. Their arguments remained the same: no parenting experience; little experience as a married couple; predictable, stress-free lifestyle; limited knowledge and familiarity with the little boy's culture; no siblings for the little boy.

Daniel questioned validity of some of these reasons. He suggested that, with the exception of the little boy wanting siblings, these reasons did not seem strong enough to deny us the opportunity to be parents to the little boy.

Daniel was still fighting to adopt the little boy. My heart broke. I had accepted that the fight for the little boy had ended. We had fought all the way to the top of the system. There was no where left to turn. Worse still, this report would be the basis of a decision regardless of who it was made by, and this report did not look favorably upon Daniel and me.

Despite everything Daniel was still fighting to adopt the little boy. I listened intently, wanting to hear any indication that there was even the smallest possibility. The smallest window of hope. Nothing.

The supervisor smiled sympathetically at Daniel. She explained that no one reason on that list was enough to deny our application to adopt the little boy, but that the accumulation of reasons and concerns had resulted in the final decision.

Final decision. Those were words I had hoped I wouldn't hear.

The man jumped in to add that he felt Daniel and I would make wonderful parents to someone, just not the little boy. I found that patronizingly ironic seeing that the report reflected no such positive feelings or notions about Daniel and me as future parents.

The supervisor and the man continued to explain. The refusal of our application had boiled down to two main issues: trust and expectations. The man maintained that it was unrealistic for Daniel and me to place any expectations on the little boy.

I struggled with this as I listened. Every child has an individual potential. Every child has the right to be believed in. There was a difference in having expectations for a child and having unrealistic expectations for a child. This conversation suggested that any expectations would be unrealistic. I was appalled. I bit back against my anger. It would take nothing for me to launch into an all out verbal attack of the report and the incompetence with which it had been written. I bit my tongue and took a deep breath. Play the game.

They continued to explain how the issue of expectations played into the little boy being better suited for a home with other children. Other children would allow the little boy to blend into the background; to not be the primary focus for his adoptive parents. Expectations of success and achievements could be placed on other siblings. The adoptive parents could live vicariously through their other children and not allow themselves to pin their hopes and dreams on the little boy.

I felt sad for the little boy. It was sad to realize that he would be placed in a family in which he could become invisible. The system would ensure that he would not run the risk of becoming the apple of anyone's eye. I thought that was terrible. I believed every child, no matter how limited in their abilities, deserved the chance to be loved and adored - to be the center of someone's universe. This wasn't anything to do with expectations; it was pure, unconditional love.

That's what Daniel and I had wanted to offer the little boy. But that was unrealistic and unwanted.

I smiled and nodded my head as they spoke. Despite their belief that I was not self-aware, I maintained my composure. The man began taking notes. This was entirely déjà vu. I was cautious not to look at the man as he took out his note pad and began jotting notes.

I knew that looking at him would feed into his already established belief that I was analyzing his every move in some attempt to maintain control of the situation. Just another presumed side effect of my infertility, their displaced knowledge infuriated me.

The supervisor talked about the second reason that Daniel and I were not considered a match for the little boy - trust. The man and the woman had felt that Daniel and I did not trust them, the process, or the system. They questioned my trust more than Daniel's. All this because I was too cold to take off my jacket. Hindsight is 20/20.

The supervisor commented on the fact that Daniel and I had spoken to both the head lady and the adoption top lady as illustrating our distrust. I found that comment intriguing as Daniel and I had only done so after having been turned down. Funny that the distrust they used to base our decision on had occurred after the decision had already been made.

I didn't understand how to play this game. How could Daniel and I argue against inaccuracies that had been created to justify their position? CYA. This meeting wasn't to discuss the report. It was to put an end to our dreams of adopting the little boy.

Daniel was beginning to see this as well. Every question he asked had a counter, and every counter he challenged led to more questions.

Daniel sat back in his chair. He was discouraged. The hopelessness was settling in.

Despite the hopelessness of the situation I attempted to address the issue of trust. Instead of replying to the supervisor I turned my attention to the man. "I apologize if you felt as though we distrusted you. We did not go to the head lady or the adoption top lady because of an issue with trust. We went to them because there was no room for discussion when we met with you and the woman. It had been stated three times, very clearly, that you were "one hundred percent confident in your decision". This was actually said as an introduction to our meeting. That statement did not open any doors for discussion. It suggested that there was no room for discussion as neither of you were willing to reconsider your positions."

I looked from the man to the supervision. She turned to look at him. He looked from me to her and back to me again. He looked somewhat surprised. "I never thought about it like that," he conceded.

The supervisor turned back to me. Aside from addressing a few of the issues Daniel had brought forward, I had yet to comment on my reaction to the report. "Morgan you must feel like this report was attacking you," the supervisor said. Her voice was sympathetic as were her eyes.

I had listened intently as Daniel had worked through his questions and concerns. I knew that their stance was not going to change. I wanted the supervisor to realize that the report was based more on insinuation than it was on facts. I needed to be careful. I knew she herself had read the report and that her thoughts of me would be biased. Play the game.

"Can I hold your hand for a second?" I asked extending my hand out toward her. The man watched me questioningly. She leaned forward and gently took my hand. "I'm freezing," I stated. "It's the middle of summer and I am absolutely freezing."

It was true. My fingers were like ice. I knew they were. I was always cold.

"I didn't take my jacket off because I was cold." I turned to the man. "You suggested that I didn't trust you. That by asking about a look you exchanged with the woman I was somehow not trusting you. Actually, I did trust you. I trusted you enough to ask. I trusted that I could ask you questions without being judged. You on the other hand did not trust me. Had you trusted me enough to ask me about my jacket I would have told you that I was cold. Not that I am guarded or suspicious or distrusting. Not that I was trying to control our meeting. I was cold."

The man looked back at me. For a moment he said nothing. Slowly he nodded his head. Point taken. I sat back in my chair and continued.

"A lot of the things in this report are based on interpretation and generalization. I'm sure that there are many times when a person leaves their coat on for all the reasons stated in that report," I said motioning to the desk where she had laid the report. "But generalizations do not apply to each and every situation. Many of the statements made in the report do not apply to Daniel and I."

I held my breath for the quickest of moments and then forged ahead. I explained about the comment regarding Daniel's father. I offered the counterpoint that Daniel had not been asked many questions about his father. The man and the supervisor just nodded. The man took notes.

I clarified the issue about my perceived need to control situations and my supposed inability to deal with emotions. I was furious, but I spoke calmly. Play the game.

I explained the differences between Daniel's personality and my own, highlighting my desire to hear everything before making decisions and Daniel's preference to ask questions as he moves through information. I pointed out the balance in our approach - the understanding we had for one another's situation-handling abilities.

I referred back to the report. I reiterated the assumptions and interpretations made in the report that suggested this was related to some deep routed emotional issues. The man continued to take notes as the supervisor took it all in.

I knew she was trying to put the things I was saying into context. Trying to match what I was saying with what she had learned about me from the report. Things didn't fit together. I was not the same psychologically challenged monster described in the report. I was presenting sincere and genuine thoughts and emotions I was described as being void of. She would have to decide for herself who I was and what that meant for the report.

The last point I clarified was the point of infertility. The entire basis of my badly misconstrued character profile.

I knew the literature on infertility and the theories about infertility and control issues and infertility and emotional blockages. I also knew from reading the report that Daniel and I had been pigeon-holed to fit those theories and then judged accordingly.

The truth of the matter was that Daniel and I differed from other couples facing infertility in one particular way. We had known about the infertility prior to marriage and had discussed our options openly.

I had been in a relationship previously in which I had learned of my infertility. I did not want Daniel to lead a childless life just because I was unable to bear children. Daniel wanted children. I knew that. We confronted this issue before our relationship became too serious. I wanted to offer Daniel the possibility of children; to allow him to gracefully and understandably bow out of a future with me in order to fulfill his desires to have children.

Daniel's love for me was strong. He wanted to build a life with me despite my issue of infertility. We knew what our options were. We would decide when the time was right whether we wanted to live childfree or whether we wanted to explore alternatives to pregnancy.

I knew nothing I said would change the report. It was final. I was, however, hoping to shed some light on the reality of who Daniel and I were. I wanted the supervisor to see the flaws in the report and begin to doubt its credibility. Not that it mattered. Daniel and I would not be offered the opportunity to adopt the little boy. I just wanted to right the wrong that been done.

Even though Daniel and I appeared to be monsters on paper, I wanted the supervisor to realize that an enormous mistake had been made. I knew it wouldn't change things for Daniel and me. I just hoped it might disallow the same mistakes from happening to other couples.

I wondered how many other couples had been in the same situation as Daniel and me. I had no idea how many there might have been or who they were - but however many there had been, and whoever they were, I felt for them.

I could have continued with my justifications and rationalizations but there was no point. All the rationalizations in the world would not re-write the report. It was what it was.

CHAPTER 15

THEIR ADVICE

THE MAN PUT HIS NOTEBOOK aside and folded his hands in his lap.

Daniel and I had said all there was to say. The supervisor was the first to speak. "Where to from here." Although it was a question, she phrased it as a statement. "Where to from here." That had been the intent of this meeting. Not to rectify any decisions or anything in the report, but to determine "what next," for Daniel and me.

I wasn't sure how to answer, although it hadn't really been a question. I didn't know where to from here. Neither did Daniel. We had tried to discuss it many times but it was very difficult to decide where to when we didn't know where we were to begin with. We had not been ready to let go of our dreams of adopting the little boy.

We had talked about putting in a general application for adoption, an application in which a child is assigned to you if you are assessed as being acceptable potential parents. Despite our desires to share our lives with children, it was hard to discuss giving up on the little boy and continuing on without him. Talking about reapplying for adoption had seemed like we were resigning ourselves to the fact that the little boy would not be a part of our family. We were not ready to accept that.

Daniel and I looked at each other.

"It is difficult to get over the loss caused by infertility," she began. I was a little taken aback. The belief that Daniel and I had not dealt with our infertility drove me crazy. We had not only dealt with it, we had accepted it as a part of who we were.

We understood that our infertility would play a role in our lives and in determining our "where to from here." We had weighed our options. We considered the pros and cons of being childless versus alternate ways of having children.

Regardless of when or where the conversations had arisen, the result was always the same. Daniel and I wanted a family.

"Many couples do not realize the grief and loss associated with infertility," she continued. I looked at Daniel. He shot me a quick, reassuring smile. He understood.

I loved Daniel. I loved how he always knew what I was thinking and feeling; and, right now, I loved that he felt just as patronized as I did. Yes we were infertile. Did they not want to at least ask us a bit about that before determining where we might be on the infertility grief scale?

I was once again caught up in the shock of how people who were allegedly trained to assess others could so quickly fall prey to generalizations, assumptions, and stereotyping.

"We have a pamphlet for couples just like you," she continued, "who come back later and thank us for the information. Many couples tell us they weren't even aware of their issues before they read the pamphlet."

"Many couples just like you." That annoyed me. No two couples are exactly alike, even the ones experiencing infertility issues.

"That sounds great," Daniel said. "Do you have a pamphlet we can take home and read?" The supervisor looked delighted by the request. I shot Daniel a quick smile. He winked at me. Play the game.

The conversation quickly took on an upbeat nature. The man reminded us once again of the many wonderful qualities Daniel and I had to offer as potential parents. The supervisor spoke about the process of reapplying for a general adoption if Daniel and I chose to pursue that option. "Of course," she added, "you'd need to take time to deal with your grief and loss first. Not only from your infertility, but from the little boy as well."

I wanted to ask exactly how long that would be before Daniel and I could reapply. I knew better than to ask though. I knew how that would look. The man and the supervisor would assume that I was denying not only the issues they felt were at hand, but also the time they deemed necessary for Daniel and me to come to terms with our issues.

"Daniel and I do want a family someday," I replied. Daniel agreed although we both maintained an air of neutral, matter-of-factness. We did not want our statements or intentions to be misunderstood and we were both very aware of how easily that could happen. The report had been proof of that.

"Well," she said very pleased with herself, "you would already be ahead of the game. The initial assessment has already been done and the report is on file and would not need to be redone."

"I think I'd rather a new report," I chuckled. Everyone laughed. We were all aware that the report was not the most glowing testament to Daniel and my attributes as future parents.

Although I had said the statement jokingly I had also meant it. The report was crap. It was a horrible misrepresentation of Daniel and me. I doubted we would be able to adopt a pet from the SPCA using that report.

"And as you know," she explained, "if you do reconsider adoption, you would have two workers assigned to your case." She continued to explain the assignment of workers and the current shortage in manpower. As it stood, we would once again be looking at a worker from our area and one from the larger city. It would not be the woman. She had retired.

"One case too late," I thought to myself.

"I would love to work with you guys again," the man said. "You guys were great." I was dumbfounded. We were "great"??? Where was all this greatness in the report? And did he seriously think we'd want to work with him again? Whether or not he was directly responsible for what was written in the report did not matter. He had agreed with it and signed his name to it. I did not like the man let alone wish to work with him again.

I looked at him curiously. He was looking back and fourth from Daniel to me. He was smiling. He clasped his hands behind his head and crossed his right leg over his left. He was completely comfortable with the idea of working with us again, and judging by his posture he had not considered that Daniel and I may have an issue working with him.

I found it ironic that I was the one who had been described as being unaware. What a boob.

I mustered up all the self-control I could find and smiled back at him. "That would be great," I said. Daniel shot me quick look of approval. Play the game.

The meeting continued to lighten up as it neared its completion. "Does anyone know what time it is?" the supervisor asked. "I don't have my watch on," replied the man. Daniel supplied the supervisor with the time as I jokingly replied to the man. "I'm not surprised. You wouldn't want the alarm to go off after last time." We all laughed. I'm sure if anyone thought about it a whole lot it would come across as passive aggressive. But for the time being we were all enjoying a bit of light humor after what could easily have become a bitter battle.

The supervisor put her hand on my shoulder as she walked us to the door. "Well," she smiled, "that went better than I expected." "I'm not surprised." I answered, "Based on the report I wouldn't have expected much either."

We shared a knowing smile. She knew that Daniel and I were not the people we had been described as in the report. I knew that she knew the difference. I also knew that it would not matter. The report was final. The decision was final. Daniel and I would not be adopting the little boy.

CHAPTER 16

WHERE TO FROM HERE

I SLID INTO THE PASSENGER seat as Daniel started the engine. I could still feel where she had placed her hand on my shoulder. "Well," I chuckled, "that went better than they expected."

Daniel smiled at me. He knew I was not waiting for a response from him. I was irate. He knew what was coming.

"Well you didn't end up sounding too overly bad," I had said. "At least in comparison anyway." That had been the opening of the flood gates. Daniel and I talked about the meeting and about the report most of the drive home. We could not get passed how off-the-mark the workers had been in their assumptions and speculations. We were frustrated that our assessment had been so badly misconstrued.

It was hard not to take things personally. It was actually impossible not to take things personal since everything in that report had been quite personal.

Daniel reached over and took my hand. He walked me through the report, explaining his insights into their blunders. He reassured me that the people we had read about were not us. I already knew that. That was what made everything so frustrating. Still, it was nice to hear Daniel verbalize the same thoughts and feelings I was experiencing.

I returned the favor. I brought up the ridiculous things that had been printed about Daniel. I was enraged that the workers had commented on Daniel's religious beliefs. I don't think anyone has the right to judge the religious beliefs of another. Besides that, it was not like Daniel was fanatical. Daniel was a Roman Catholic, as was I, and according to the Roman Catholic Church, fertilization outside of natural conception is a mortal sin. There is nothing naïve about that.

I also felt badly for the comment about Daniel and his father. The comment had implied that there was some deep-rooted issue that needed probing. That could not be further from the truth. Daniel loved and respected both his parents. There were no hidden issues that needed to be unearthed.

I informed Daniel that I felt the report had been a pile of crap and that the comment about his father had not stemmed from anything he had said.

I knew Daniel well enough to know that he would be wondering if he had said something that may have been interpreted as an issue between him and his father. It would bother him if that were the case. But honestly and truly this was not the case and I told Daniel that.

On the bright side, if there were such a thing in this particular situation, so much of the report was so far from the truth that it was easy for Daniel and I to recognize that the issue had not been us. We had not been turned down because of who we were. We had been turned down because of who they depicted us to be.

Again I wondered how many other couples had experienced the same injustice.

I wondered what this meant for the little boy. My heart ached for him. Daniel and I would have loved to share our hearts and our home with him. If only things had been different. If only things had been seen for what they were. If only we could have known how our every word would be misinterpreted and misconstrued. If only. If only.

I could feel Daniel's eyes on me. I had been quite for the last few miles. I had been contemplating all the "if onlys" that had happened. I smiled up at him. I was devastated and heartbroken. Things seemed so final.

"So," I began, "where to from here?"

It was Daniel's turn to be quiet. His brows tightened slightly and he chewed on his thumbnail. He often chewed his nails when he was deep in thought.

"I don't know," he said finally.

"Is it over?" I didn't want to ask the question and somewhere deep inside I was sure I didn't want to hear the answer. It had been pretty clear in the meeting. The little boy was not an option. Other options were presented and discussed, but of course Daniel and I would have to come to grips with our infertility first.

"She didn't give us the pamphlet," I stated.

"We'll have to call her and ask for it," Daniel said thoughtfully. His brows knit together tighter. He took his thumb away from his mouth and smiled. "Yes," he said. "We'll have to call her and ask for it."

I looked at him quizzically. I knew he was deliberating on our where to from here but I wasn't sure exactly where he was going. He glanced at me and grinned.

"If they say we need to deal with things, we'll deal with them. If they say we need to read the pamphlet, we'll read the pamphlet. There's no point in trying to tell them we've already dealt with things, they've decided otherwise. So, we'll play the game. If they think reading the pamphlet will help then we'll read the pamphlet and tell them how wonderful and helpful it was. They said couples are always so thankful. We'll be thankful. We'll be whatever they want us to be. We'll play the game."

I smiled at Daniel. I loved his optimism and his enthusiasm. I slid closer to him and rested my head on his shoulder. He wrapped his arm around my shoulders and entwined his fingers in mine.

"If I really am a monster I hope you would tell me," I said thinking back to the report.

"Not even close," he said leaning over to kiss the top of my head. "Not even close."

We were quiet for the rest of the drive home. The meeting had been mentally exhausting and we were both worn out. I couldn't wait to get home and curl up on the couch next to Daniel. Of course before we'd do that we'd need to call our families. They were waiting anxiously to find out about our meeting.

Each phone call resulted in the same shock and disgust Daniel and I had felt. Our families were as angry and confused as we were. No one had expected the meeting to have gone the way it had. Everyone had been holding out hope that the supervisor would see what was going on and reverse the decision. However wonderful that hope had been, that was not the case.

Daniel and I took comfort in our families' reactions. It was somewhat settling to realize that other people disagreed with the things that had been written in the report as much as we did. In some strange way it put our minds at ease - reassured us that we had not overreacted.

My aunt had cried when I had told her about our meeting. She had been holding out so much hope for Daniel and I and the little boy. Her heart was broken for us. She felt betrayed by the system that she herself had once worked for. She struggled to understand how wrong things had ended up for us. She searched for the right thing to say. There was no right thing to say. Daniel and I both understood that.

CHAPTER 17

THE GAME

DANIEL AND I WAITED A few days and then sent the supervisor an e-mail. We thanked her for the meeting and expressed our gratitude for her taking the time to sit and talk with us. We acknowledged how much it meant for us to receive clarity and closure.

We ended the e-mail by requesting the infertility pamphlet she had recommended. We explained that we were ready to move forward and wanted to address any obstacles standing in our way.

In less than a week a large brown envelope appeared in the mail. It had both our names written on it and the stamp in the top left corner confirmed that it had come from the supervisor.

Daniel and I were returning home from grocery shopping when we stopped to pick up the mail. I picked the envelope from the pile of fliers and waved it at him. Let the games begin.

I slowly opened the large envelope. I felt strange; hollow. Although everything we were doing was part of a larger plan to prove ourselves to the supervisor and the man, the process seemed empty without the possibility of the little boy. Playing the game seemed pointless if the little boy was no longer an option for us.

I sighed as I pulled the pamphlet out of the envelope. Pamphlet was an understatement. The content of the envelope was actually a nineteen page article. At the top of the page, in big beautiful cursive font was the word "Understanding." Underneath that; centered and in bold caps were the words: A GUIDE TO IMPAIRED FERTILITY FOR FAMILY AND FRIENDS. Impaired fertility. Even that was patronizing.

The article was written for family and friends of couples suffering with what the author referred to as impaired fertility. It began by introducing the concept of infertility and explaining what exactly that meant and where the medical society was with possible interventions. The author cautions family and friends to be realistic and not to give the couple any false hope as this will only serve to support the couple's denial.

From there the article outlines the emotional stages the couple must pass through in order to effectively deal with their infertility. The stages included: surprise, denial, isolation, anger, grief, depression, and acceptance. Next the author describes how many couples find themselves stuck in a particular stage and have to work hard to overcome that stage and progress through the remaining stages. At that point the couple is then able to consider their other alternatives: adoption, choosing a childfree lifestyle, advanced medical options.

Daniel and I read through the pamphlet. The information was not new, and the stages were something we had progressed through early in our marriage. Despite where we were or weren't, the man and his supervisor did not recognize this. They believed that because we were infertile, we were somehow impaired and in need of fixing.

"Therapy is an option. Of course, we are not able to provide this, but there are many trained therapists who could help you through the grieving process." She smiled that empathetic smile, believing she understood our pain.

I gritted my teeth. Infertile does not mean impaired. Daniel and I had moved passed the grieving period. The fact that we were there, seeking to adopt was proof that we had already accepted our lives and were moving forward. I didn't understand how they didn't get that.

It was frustrating that the man and woman hadn't even touched on our fertility issues during the home study, but had written their assumptions into the report. It was also frustrating to realize that any attempt Daniel and I made to clarity our acceptance of our infertility was chalked up to denial. It was an infuriating cycle.

I took a deep breath and unclenched my jaw. I smiled. Play the game.

"We would definitely be interested in any materials you might have," Daniel had said. Had this been a game of tennis I would have given him a high-five for the nice return. Daniel was a great player; and we were definitely going to have to play their game if we had any hope of adopting the little boy.

"Learn anything new?" I asked. "Nope," Daniel answered, "but we should definitely send them an e-mail thanking them for the pamphlet and telling them how helpful it was." "Still playing are we?" I asked with a smile.

We hadn't talked about the little boy in a while. We had both left the last meeting feeling very hopeless. The man and his supervisor had moved on. The little boy had not been the topic of the meeting. The option of applying for a general adoption had been their focus.

The little boy needed a home with siblings; and they needed a couple who trusted them completely in order to move forward. My heart had closed in that meeting and I had to swallow hard to get rid of the lump in my throat.

"It's not over till it's over. Isn't that what you always say?" Daniel smiled at me and put his arm around my shoulders. It felt nice to snuggle close to him. It felt nice to share our dream about the little boy, despite how bleak that reality was.

Daniel and I sent the e-mail later that afternoon. We thanked the supervisor for all her help - for meeting with us and mailing us the package. We commented on how helpful the information had been and how much conversation and soul-searching it had generated for us.

At that point the ball was in their court. We would have to wait for her reply before deciding on our next move. Waiting was always difficult. But it was something we had gotten good at doing.

CHAPTER 18

A SIBLING FOR THE LITTLE BOY

WE DIDN'T HEAR BACK FROM the supervisor for the rest of the week; not that we had expected to. Time always seemed to drag on when we were on the waiting end of things. We used to spend our time talking and dreaming and making plans for the future. This time was different. We weren't so much talking and dreaming as we were planning and strategizing. Instead of discussing possible family outings and new traditions, we were discussing next moves and best counters.

Now that we knew the reasons we had not been selected as a match for the little boy we could begin to rectify those issues. We had already begun to establish a relationship of trust with the man and the supervisor. We had agreed to working with the man again in the future and we had openly requested and accepted materials they felt we needed. We were appreciative of their suggestions and did our best to jump through every hoop they presented.

Siblings for the little boy would be harder to achieve. We knew that Daniel's nieces were not enough, despite their closeness both in proximity and relationships. That was the obstacle. We couldn't get around that. We didn't have children and so siblings were just not possible. Maybe someday we would have children; after all we were in the class of unexplained infertility which does not conclusively rule out conception. It just makes the odds really, really improbable.

We had been walking through one of the larger malls in the city. Just walking and talking. As we walked along hand-in-hand we talked through our thoughts and issues. Despite our conversations we kept coming back to that one stumbling block - siblings for the little boy. We knew we would need to resolve all the issues surrounding the adoption of the little boy if we were to have any hope at all of having them reconsider their decision. But each and every time we came to the issues of siblings it was like a dead-end. There was just no getting around it. No matter which way we looked at it we could not overcome that criterion.

I don't know where our next thought came from. I don't know if it had been Daniel's idea or my own. But suddenly we were discussing the possibility of adopting two children - the little boy and an older child. We wondered if this would even be possible.

If the little boy would do better in a home with an older child, we would do our best to provide that. We would talk to the man and his supervisor. We would ask that they choose an older child who would make a great match for the little boy. Perhaps if they had the control of matching his siblings they would be more interested and empowered to help us.

The more we discussed the idea the more excited we became. Adopting two children at the same time would eliminate any feelings of inferiority between the children and would connect them through experience. They would be coming into our family together; as equals. There would be no preconceived favorites or issues of territorialism. They would come into our family together and we would all grow together as one unit.

Daniel and I were both very excited about the idea. We had always dreamed about having a family - and that dream was never limited to one child. I couldn't believe the idea hadn't dawned on us earlier. We certainly had the room in our home and in our hearts for two children. We had no expectations or pre-determined criteria for either child. We already loved the little boy, and we knew we would love whatever child was chosen to be his older sibling be it a brother or a sister.

The more I thought about it the more I realized the idea wasn't entirely new. Daniel had enquired about the little boy's biological siblings in our third meeting. He had been willing to consider the idea of opening our home to the little boy's sisters and brothers if they had been in need of a home.

"They don't want to be adopted," the woman had said coolly. "They are just waiting until they

are old enough to go back to their mother." She always seemed so defensive when she spoke about the little boy's biological family. We knew she was the worker for the mother and the siblings, but we were always surprised by how much this affected her work with us. I often wondered how this was not seen as a conflict of interest.

I questioned what went through the man's mind. Did he hear the defensive tone in her voice? Did he recognize her obvious bias in favor of the little boy's mother? I wondered if he ever brought this up after the fact. Did he discuss it with her, or with his superiors?

And what about the time she had come right out and expressed her sympathies for the little boy's mother? "If you don't feel sorry for her then you aren't capable of open adoption." That was a pretty big statement. That was a pretty big croc of shit. Daniel and I were more than willing to facilitate any relationships necessary for the little boy's personal development. We were not, however, willing to feel sorry for someone who allowed such horrible things to happen to a young child. Overlook for his best interest - yes; forgive and forget - never.

It had been a while since I had felt the warm flicker of hope stirring inside me. Its passion and energy were a welcome and familiar feeling. My soul felt light and my heart felt happy. We had found a loop hole, and in doing so, we had found a way to keep our dream alive.

I practically skipped through the parking lot with Daniel close in tow. We were as light on our feet as we were in spirit. It is said that anything worth your love is worth your fight. Perhaps this is true. Daniel and I had certainly been through a long and drawn out battle. And as hopeless as it had looked at times here we were, still fighting.

I was almost giddy as we drove home. We dreamed about life with children - life with the little boy and whoever else would comprise our family. We delighted in the thought of our family, whether it be two boys or a boy and a girl. We fantasized about holidays and vacations and Christmases to come... the pitter patter of feet running through the house, the familiar squabble of siblings when play had gotten out of hand, the bedtime rituals of stories and kisses.

The ride home was wonderful. Our newly founded hope had ignited a whole new world of dreams - dreams we had never conceived of.

It was nice to have hope, to dare once again to dream. As fantastical as that day was, we knew there would be many struggles along the way; not the least of them being the waiting. We knew from our experience thus far that adoption was not a quick process. Adoption took months and sometimes years to complete.

"This doesn't just happen overnight," the woman snapped. Her voice was agitated. We hadn't meant to suggest that things should happen so quickly. We were just curious about how the process worked and what to expect next.

The man jumped in. "First you fill in the forms, then you go through the necessary requirements-criminal record check, medical record check, and all that. Then you go through the adoption training and if there are any issues that stand out you get those resolved. So, for example a couple may have to go through financial counseling or family counseling or something if those are areas of need. Then there is the matching process where your profile would be matched to that of a child, and then the actual relationship building takes a long time. You start out by exchanging letters and pictures. Then you might share videos and talk on the phone. Then you'd have arranged, supervised visits at the foster home and then later at your home. Eventually the child would have some things left at your house and longer visits would happen. You would work your way into sleep-overs and then eventually you would be ready for the adoption. The relationship building is really important so it does take a long time."

Daniel and I both knew things would not happen quickly. We also knew that we were in it for the long haul and that we would wait as long as we had to. Having a family was not something that would happen overnight and we knew that. We knew the steps involved in making our family a reality and we were ready for that.

CHAPTER 19

APPLYING AGAIN

SUMMER WAS COMING TO A quick end and Daniel and I were once again back to work. Our new jobs found us closer to the big city. We planned on picking up the application form the first week back. We were not sure if we would need two, one for the little boy and one for his potential sibling, or if we would just need one for the new child we planned to adopt. We decided to pick up one form and include a letter of intent.

We wanted to talk to the man and his supervisor before we sent in our application. We did not want them to feel as if we had gone over their heads. We wanted to include them in every step of the process. Having them as allies would be far more beneficial than having them as opponents.

It had been a little over a month since we had seen them last. Although the report had been terrible we had done our best to end that meeting on a positive note. We had also been in contact with the supervisor regarding the infertility package and that correspondence had all been upbeat and encouraging.

The first few days of work had been hectic, but our top priority was still our family. We had designated Friday night as our evening to fill out the application form and draft our letter of intent. Once we knew what our application entailed and had an idea of what we were putting in our letter we would then call to set up and appointment with the man and his supervisor.

Filling out the application was bitter sweet. We had been through so much since the last application. But the idea of moving ahead and creating our family kept our spirits high. The application was the easy part, at least easy relative to the letter.

The application consisted of page after page of checklists. Although each question prompted discussion between Daniel and me, the process of checking the boxes was not a difficult one. Daniel and I knew we wanted to share our lives; we were ready to move from being a couple to having a family. We knew we wanted to share our lives with the little boy, and we were excited to add a second child to that dream.

We were not specific on the application as to any criteria for the second child. We felt it would be more beneficial to allow the man and his supervisor to be a large part of that decision. They knew what they were looking for in terms of a family for the little boy. By allowing them to determine a match for the little boy's sibling we were hoping they would feel connected and committed to our family.

That's why the letter would be so important. Putting that in just the right words would be difficult. We didn't want the man and his supervisor to feel as though we were trying to manipulate them in any way. And Daniel and I were not interested in building a family through manipulation. We wanted to work with the man and his supervisor, despite everything we had been through, to build a family that would work for us as well as for them. And even more importantly, with their support we knew our family would be designed to work for the little boy as well as our other child; whoever he or she may be.

Daniel and I loved to talk about our future family. We wondered if our second child would be older or younger. We both assumed older as it had been discussed in our earlier meetings that the little boy would benefit from a household with older children. We wondered if the child would be a brother or a sister; a son or a daughter.

We had no expectations or limitations. We were opened to any child chosen to be a part of our family. We needed to be clear in our letter that we would love any child chosen to complete our family; boy or girl, older or younger. And, most importantly, we needed to be clear that we were willing to work through any issues necessary to ensure a healthy start for our family.

Daniel and I were willing to undergo any therapy we needed; individually and as a couple. We were willing to attend family counseling session to prepare us for life with a family. We were willing to attend any and every workshop available to new parents, to adoptive parents, and to families in general. We were also committed to providing counseling opportunities for our children, and to attending counseling as a new family.

We knew that there would be many bumps ahead of us, but we also knew that we would learn as we went. Daniel and I both believed that the key to a healthy family was the ability to communicate openly. Through open communication we could develop trust and establish relationships.

We knew this would not happen over night. It would take a long time for each of us, adults and children, to adapt to our new lives and to establish ourselves and our roles within our new family unit. Love takes time. Trust takes time. Relationships take time. Daniel and I were willing to dedicate the rest of our lives to all of these things which we hoped would become the cornerstones of our family.

So. The letter had to be perfect. We knew exactly what we wanted to say, but we also knew how easily things could be misinterpreted and misconstrued. This was our last chance. Our only hope of building a family that would include the little boy rested on the outcome of our letter and our proposal to build a family together with the man and his supervisor.

It had been a month and a half since our last visit with them. Despite how well it ended there was still a lot of water under the bridge, especially for Daniel and me. Our thoughts and words had been used against us in the past. We needed to ensure that our letter could be viewed only as positive. As two people wanted and willing to share their lives. Two people willing to make every effort to create a family in which two children could grow up feeling loved, supported, and cherished. Two children. The little boy and whomever else we would be blessed enough to adopt.

CHAPTER 20

THE LETTER

DANIEL AND I SAT IN front of the computer with our completed application in hand. We had gone over it what felt like a million times. We wanted it to be perfect. It would be pretty hard to mess up a checklist; but still, the hopes and dreams of our future family depended on this application and the letter we were about to create.

We had gone over the details many times. We wanted to begin our letter with an explanation about our situation to date. We wanted to include a brief summary of our first attempt to adopt the little boy and the reasons why we were not deemed suitable. The wording for this would be tricky. We would need to ensure that our words were not judgmental or accusatory. Our words needed to express our genuine desire to meet the needs of the little boy with the help and support of the agency.

Then we needed to delicately bridge into the idea of adopting the little boy and a second child. We also needed to explain and support how adopting two children would alleviate many of the concerns about the little boy being an only child. Somewhere we would need to include our desire to have the agency match a second child to our family. We wanted our letter to ensure that whoever ended up reading this letter felt empowered; felt a sense of ownership and commitment to the creation of our family.

It would be important to end our letter emphasizing how we were willing to do anything and everything possible to help facilitate this.

Daniel and I both knew our family would only be a possibility if the top adoption person, whoever took over since the top lady retired, bought into the idea. Deep breath.

I looked over at Daniel. He looked back at me. My heart was thumping inside my chest and my hands felt sweaty. This reminded me so much of all the meetings we had had before. I was reminded of sitting in the waiting room, and then in that little office. Most of all I was reminded of that small sterile room. The room we had been taken to before March Break. The room where my heart had shattered and my stomach had crawled up into my throat. Deep breath.

This was it. This letter would end things one way or the other. It was our last chance. I took one last deep breath. Click. The monitor lit up and awaited instructions. Deep breath.

I doubled clicked on the word processor and then rubbed my hands together. They were cold and clammy. I was nervous.

I peeked up at Daniel. He was looking at the monitor and his jaw seemed tight. I knew he was as nervous as I was. At least we had time on our side. We could write our letter and then edit it a thousand times if we needed to. But still we were nervous.

I chewed nervously on my lip as I waited for the program to load. Old computers drive me crazy. We really needed a new one. This computer had been around for nearly a decade and had fulfilled its duty beyond every expectation. I sent it a silent thank you as the CPU hummed to life.

I leaned my head on Daniel's shoulder as we waited. I felt a little less nervous. "I love you," I told him. "I love you too," he said as he turned his head to kiss my forehead. Just breath.

"Well," he said as the word processor opened up, "this is it." "This is it," I agreed.

We stared at the blank screen in silence. What should we say? How should we start? Dear sir/madame? To whom it may concern? Both seemed impersonal. I sat back in the chair and leaned against Daniel once again. Deep breath.

"Well," I said, "here we go." I sat back up and poised my hands over the keyboard. A million things ran through my head but none of them made their way to the keyboard. I closed my eyes and pictured the little boy. I felt a smile tugging on the corners of my mouth as a warm tingle made its way through my veins. My heart seemed to slow to a normal pace in response and my body relaxed.

Words filled the page as Daniel and I took turns verbalizing our most intimate thoughts and feelings. We translated our hopes and dreams into words and wove them throughout our letter. We poured our hearts and souls into the letter.

I looked up at Daniel. His eyes moved from the monitor and met mine. I raised my eyebrows at him. "Well?" I asked, "think we got a shot?" Daniel didn't answer right away. How could he? We had thought we had a shot so many times before that it was nearly impossible to believe that this time might be different.

Daniel looked back at the monitor and tilted his head. His eyebrows knit together ever so slightly, the way they do when he is contemplating something. "Yah," he said finally. "I really think we do."

I exhaled long and deep. I hadn't realized that I had been holding my breath. Daniel reached down and took my hand. I sat back and leaned into him once again. We fell silent as we read and re-read our letter.

We made a few minor changes but all in all we were pleased with the outcome. This letter was the most sincere and honest demonstration of our hopes, our dreams, and more importantly, ourselves, than we had ever been able to achieve before. We knew there would still be a lot of work to do, but we were confident that our letter would be a new beginning.

CHAPTER 21

NEW BEGINNINGS

DANIEL AND I TOOK A break from the computer. We wanted to come back to our letter with fresh eyes and minds before we contacted the man and his supervisor to set up an appointment. We still wanted to involve them from the very beginning. We wanted to go over our application and our letter with them before sending it off for final judgment.

We decided to celebrate our rekindled hope by going out to eat. It had felt like ages since Daniel and I had done anything like that. Our last weeks and months had been so busy and so emotionally draining that even our down time had provided little reprieve.

We talked excitedly over dinner, once again daring to share the "what ifs" of our future family. It was nice. Daniel and I had a really great time. Things seemed so natural, so unencumbered.

We took the long way home, following the ocean as long as possible. We felt the wind in our hair and smelled the saltwater. It was a beautiful day.

The entire summer had been quite nice actually. We had experienced record temperatures and rain only seemed to happen late into the night. Daniel and I had been on an emotional roller-coaster for most of the summer and had little opportunity to take advantage of the beautiful weather.

Daniel took a right turn a mile before our home. I smiled over at him. It was as if he had been reading my mind. I knew exactly where he was going. There was a beach just a few miles down the road.

I took Daniel's hand as I slid across the seat and hopped down from behind the steering wheel. We walked hand in hand along the beach. I closed my eyes and tilted my face to the sun as we walked along. Daniel guided me past rocks and the occasional mound of seaweed. We sat down on a huge rock which jutted out from the cape. Everything about this day was beautiful.

It had been so long since Daniel and I had stopped to enjoy life - to enjoy each other. We laid back against the rock and felt the spray from the waves dance gently around us. The moist air felt nice against my skin. "Thank you," I whispered smiling. Daniel squeezed my hand softly in response.

We returned home a few hours later. We were still laughing and talking as we sat down to our letter. We read through it carefully one final time. Neither Daniel nor I made any changes. The letter was perfect.

We decided we would e-mail the man's supervisor to set up the meeting. Based on past experience it was safe to conclude that a phone call would result in a prolonged game of phone tag.

I took a deep breath and rubbed my hands together eagerly. Daniel gave my shoulder a reassuring squeeze. This was it. I doubled clicked on the e-mail icon and we waited patiently for the program to respond.

I logged into my hotmail account and was surprised to find an e-mail there from a colleague of ours. The title was "thought you should know." Daniel and I decided to read that e-mail first so that we'd be able to then concentrate fully on our task at hand. Otherwise it would drive me crazy wondering what exactly it was we "should know." Daniel was the same way. So, it was a relatively easy decision to take a quick peek at that e-mail first.

I clicked open the e-mail and Daniel and I both read in silence. I don't know how long it took Daniel to read the e-mail. I hadn't looked at him. I had just sat there staring at the screen in shocked disbelief. He was gone. Our little boy had been adopted almost a month ago.

I felt betrayed. The man and the woman had told us countless times how adoption didn't happen quickly. How it takes many months to adopt a child after a match has been identified. We had been in an office with the man and his supervisor only a month before the little boy had been officially adopted. They would have known he was in the process of being adopted. They would have known he was not available to become part of a family with Daniel and me. Why hadn't they told us?

We both understood about confidentially. We would never have expected to learn who was adopting the little boy, but just to know a match had been identified would have made our experience so much more humane. We sat in an office only five months earlier where we had been told that a successful match had not been determined. I didn't understand how any of this was possible.

"Why hadn't they just told us?" I said in a distant, almost monotone voice. "I don't know," Daniel responded softly. "They would have had to have known," I said. "I know," he responded putting his hand on my shoulder and resting his chin lightly on my head. He rubbed his thumb gently up and down the back of my neck.

My heart ached and my eyes burned. "I love him," I whispered. "Yah. Me too," replied Daniel, his voice growing hoarse. "I think I'll probably always love him," I said quietly.

I re-read the e-mail a second time before tears spilled down my face. I looked up at Daniel. He smiled down at me. There was really nothing else either of us could say. We had wanted so much for the little boy to have his happily ever after and now he would finally get that chance.

"I'm glad he finally has a forever home," Daniel whispered. "Me too," I said. I turned back to read the e-mail one final time. Tears streamed freely down my face as I laughed and sobbed at the same time. Although my heart was heavy, I could not have been happier for our little boy.

I was not crying over the loss of the little boy who I had been thinking of as my own. My tears were a reaction to what I had read; the little boy was happy. Our colleague had seen him with his new adoptive family and her e-mail had described him as smiling, as laughing, and as talking. He was talking. Our little boy was talking. He was smiling and laughing and talking. He was relaxed and happy. He had his arm wrapped around his new big brother's neck and they were both absolutely beaming.

Our little boy's adoptive family were as happy as he was. They were going to be a wonderful and happy family. They were going to create memories, share moments, and have happy times - all the things Daniel and I had been told were impossible.

They had been wrong. It had not unrealistic to want a happy life for him. And although it is not with us, Daniel and I both wish our little boy every happiness life has to offer.